'An Old Westmoi land Garage'
The Story behind Crabtree's of Kendal

By Bernard Crabtree

Edited and compiled by Anne Bonney

With acknowledgement to the assistance of the Curwen Archives Trust

Front cover photo: Z Crabtree & Co - 1923
G Wynspeare Herbert, Castle Studio, Kendal

Dedicated to my dear late wife, Laura, my son Peter and particularly
my daughter, Christine, for her unending help and support

Published by Helm Press
10 Abbey Gardens, Natland, Kendal, Cumbria LA9 7SP
Tel: 015395 61321

First Published 2000
Typeset in
Classic Garamond 10.5pt

ISBN   0 9531836 6 1

Typeset and printed by Miller Turners Ltd
The Sidings, Beezon Fields, Kendal, Cumbria, LA9 6BL Tel: 01539 740937

CONTENTS

INTRODUCTION

This is a most unusual and interesting biography of a Yorkshire family from 1880 up to the 1990s. Yorkshire folk have a reputation for being forthright and hard working - this family no exception!

It has taken me many years to get all this information gathered and put down on paper. As the reader will see and I trust appreciate, the very early writings were not witnessed by me - I wasn't yet born but it does give much information on how a struggling family existed (at least in the very early years when Zenas Crabtree left school to go into industry - he could not read - he was born about the year 1880 and life from then on was a struggle). Note, this does not infer that in 1931 or anywhere near to then that he was still unable to read and write. This had already been corrected in the early 1900s.

I did not know until about 1931 that my father had been unable to write and spell until, quite by accident, I came across two piles of books in the dark attic which were monthly issues of the Harmsworth Self Educator. These books enabled him to speak and write intelligently. It rather appears that what education he had assimilated was almost entirely numeracy, without which he must have realised that he would not get very far going into engineering. The fact that he did undoubt-edly succeed, illustrates just how successful his self-education had been. This makes me understand why he put so much pressure upon me to win a scholarship to Kendal Grammar School (now Kirkbie Kendal). He wanted me to have the best education, which at that time I don't think he would have been able to afford.

His success is undoubted and has been obtained 'the hard way' and I appreciate greatly what he did for our family. Certainly his grip on mathematics was splendid, he used micrometer readings down to 0.0009 (one ten thousandth of an inch) what is more, precision was his forte - as I believe one will understand from various sections in the text of this volume. We three lads, myself, Malcolm and Bryan owe an irredeemable debt to his most industrious life, from being a barber's lather boy at eight years of age - right through his life. We have enjoyed pleasures that would not have been available to us e.g. we all owned our own cars and houses - apart from Malcolm who died in an unfortunate motorcycling accident at nineteen and who literally 'never had the chance'.

I am now in my nineties and I have tried to write this as accurately as I can remember, so please excuse any slight errors I may have made. Photos not credited to any one person are from my own collection.

Bernard A.Crabtree

Spring 2000

Bernard in his late 40s

Fustian cutters at work for Joseph Crabtree. Taken on 26th September 1866. Abraham Crabtree, Edward Greenwood, William Lord, Thomas Greenwood and Jonathan Greenwood. Smallest apprentice name not known.

MY FOREFATHERS

My grandfather, Joseph Crabtree, was a Yorkshireman, born mid-19th century, at Hebden Bridge, in the West Riding of Yorkshire, and lived at 13 Zion Terrace with his wife, my grandmother. I only ever heard her addressed as 'Ma', although I believe her name was Mary. They had three children, Norris, the eldest, Eunice next and my father Zenas, the youngest. Norris was ten years older than Zenas and five years older than Eunice. My father got his name from the Bible, Titus chapter 3, verse 13.

Hebden Bridge is the town where folks are reputed to have looked down the chimneys of the properties below, so steep are the slopes of the valley. Zion Terrace is just such a one, it should have been named 'Suicide Terrace' because if anyone had dared to climb over the railing at the bottom of the garden, it would have been certain death. They certainly made the most of the land in Hebden Bridge and the building of massive retaining walls was commonplace. I think Zion Terrace must have been at least twenty-five feet above the street below and even that street was ten feet above the adjacent street.

My grandfather, Joseph, worked most of his life in the fustian and velveteen trade. He worked for Nut Clough's, which was situated adjacent to the River Hebden from which it got its power. It was a large factory and modern in its concept at that time. Grandfather was a 'cutter' and cut the flutes in the fustian (cutting the velvet into strips the full length of the 'piece') to make it into corduroy. His daughter, Eunice, also worked there but as a 'mender'. Occasionally the cutter went right through the cloth and that meant that it had to be repaired and she was one of the menders who made it like new again. Corduroy was popular then as it was a hard-wearing material and easily washed when soiled. Both jobs were skilled and required precision and patience.

There was another street above Zion Terrace, which was reached by some thirty-five steps and the Zion Chapel was there. My grandparents were what was called in those days 'in straightened circumstances' - they were in a biggish house and, besides her own job at the mill, Eunice used to keep the Chapel clean and tidy and delivered hot Sunday lunches to the minister and his assistants. In the 1880-90s there was little reward for the working classes and scraping a living was very difficult - there was no dole or national assistance.

Grandfather and his daughter retired about the same time, he about the age of eighty-five. Grandmother died about this time and grandfather five years later.

Norris was a bit of a loner I believe and after leaving school he went south, working his way from job to job, eventually settling in Reading. He learned his engineering skills at Thornycrofts who were internationally renowned and made lorries, coaches, fire engines and ships. The whole of his working life it could be said was at Thornycrofts and at the Herbert Engineering Company, the maker of the HE car up to about 1922. These were well constructed, though a fairly expensive four-seater car of ample proportions and very similar in appearance to the Vauxhall 14 of those pre-WW1 days. I have seen and actually worked on cars of this make after I started work in my capacity as a motor mechanic after the end of WW1.

Norris continued there until the firm folded between the wars (when their cars were out-priced) and he returned to Thornycrofts until almost the end of WW2, although by this time he must have reached the age of seventy-five. I remember this because my father telephoned him to ask, "If Thornycrofts are disposing of any of their Capstan lathes, would they send one to Kendal?" as our wartime contracts demanded a machine of this capacity. Unfortunately, due to enemy U-boats, very many of the machines went to the bottom of the Atlantic and we did not in fact receive one until 1945. We never got it into production - it was about worn out and, although we got the countershaft and other items in position, we had not really got the machine in good enough condition to manufacture work up to the standards to which we were accustomed.

When father was eight years old he went to work for a local barber as a lather boy. Safety razors had not come on the market at that time (invented 1903) and men on their way to work would nip into their regular barber's shop for a quick shave, with one of the old type 'cut throat' razors. With a lather boy preparing the next face, the barber could get through twice the number of shaves in a given time. I have no idea what the pay was but it would be minimal, valuable nonetheless in helping to feed all the family.

That job lasted, as I understand it, until Zenas was about twelve when the take-home pay was not considered to be sufficient. He later went to work in a shop in Hebden Bridge where they made wooden patterns for the engineering trade. He trained there for a while until a 'better job' was found for him as a trainee (apprentice) pattern maker with Pickles Engineering Works in Halifax. I suppose he would have gone to Halifax by train - 'buses were not on the local scene in those days, unless they were horse-drawn conveyances. He picked up pattern-making using hardwoods and sometimes knot-free sugar pine for jobs where knots could not be tolerated. He had a good journeyman pattern maker to work with. Father must have been a natural at this precise job, he quickly learned about angles, radii measurements and the contraction of metals on cooling, so much so in fact that somehow, possibly through talk in the pubs (yes, men drank in those days too but the price of beer was only pence per pint at that time), and talk about the ability of the new apprentice pattern maker and his rapid understanding of the principles of pattern making - including the allowance for the contraction of castings when cooling, which he'd quickly understood and taken into account, including the fact that not all metals contracted at the same rate when cooling. In fact, I well remember my father's steel ruler which had four scales engraved thereon - standard, contraction, double contraction and contraction for brass, there was yet another separate contraction for aluminium which was coming into general use and later it became one of the most important metals in the foundry trade.

As I said, the net result of his proficiency became widely known and even by the turn of the century he was being 'head hunted' by engineering firms from many miles away. He was eventually induced by Gardners of Patricroft, Manchester, who were making a name for themselves in the manufacture of internal combustion engines, which involved core boxes and other methods of pattern making that enabled water jackets to surround the cylinder heads and even the valve ports. Failures in foundry work of such an intricate nature were frequent and costly, so precision and great understanding of the strains in contraction of the cooling castings, were of paramount importance to the success of the whole enterprise.

Victrix Motor Works, Lound Road, Kendal about 1906

Kendal - Lound Street
Workshop early 1900s

My father must have earned recognition for his skilful work and he can only have been at Gardners for four or five years, when Mr C H Oliverson, who was interested in making light cars under the name 'Victrix', had built a small factory in Lound Road, Kendal, under that name in the early 1900s. This was a largely corrugated, ironclad building on a steel frame erected next to the Kendal Grammar School (now Kirkbie Kendal). The building was complete with loading bay which enabled incoming goods to be off-loaded at the same height as the factory floor, some two and a half feet higher than the outside roadway. A horizontal gas engine was installed and supplied by town gas for driving the machinery.

At that time Kendal was in a busy but declining wool trade, with several mills in and around the town manufacturing high quality woollen cloth, much of which was dyed in Kendal Green, a distinctive colour derived, I am told, from vegetation in the district. Most of these mills were large enough to support their own mechanics to keep the looms running. They carried out mechanical maintenance and also made parts for replacement of machine breakages and even to devise and make many of their own parts and improvements on the originals. There was in Ann Street, at this time, a millwright named Wright, Heap and Westwood, who specialised in repairing machines used in the woollen trade.

In order to make progress, Mr Oliverson required the services of a skilled pattern maker and, living in Southport, he was frequently in Manchester for the purpose of obtaining supplies of machines and tools and eventually learned of my father and his excellent work at Gardners.

I understand my father was not very satisfied with his digs in Manchester and that he, by this time, was also interested in obtaining a move and getting married to his fiancée, Edith Ashworth, who was the tenth child of Squire (Christian name) and Charlotte Ashworth of Peckett Well, near Hebden Bridge. She was one of eleven children - Charlotte, Zipporah, Victoria, Janey, Annie, Lavinia,William, Herbert, Bessie, Robert and Edith. Edith was an assistant school teacher at

C H Oliverson stand with two models of the Victrix car, on show at Southport Show.

Waterhouse & Field, 195 Lord Street, Southport

Wainsgate Church School. Lavina died of typhoid when in her late teens. Bessie was a total invalid for at least twenty years with arthritis, her hands being so bad she could not even feed herself. She was a permanent invalid from about the age of forty in Birch Hill Hospital. Robert, I believe, was a painter and decorator.

From this pool of skilled staff that Mr Oliverson had gathered, through scouts who were on the look-out for him, men were found who were willing to move into a new business in Kendal, that was going to manufacture cars in Lound Road. Walter Bare, George Bare and Walter Killingbeck were recruited and they set to work from sketches and designs provided by Mr Oliverson. My father, working to rough drawings and ideas (as distinct from the precise and accurate blue-prints of his previous employers) made patterns for the cast-iron crank cases and the water-jacketed single cylinder. I understand the crankshafts and the connecting rods were 'bought in'. Castings were made from the various patterns by Henry Rishton, whose large foundry was situated to the east of Stricklandgate, where the Westmorland Shopping Centre now stands. They were in their day excellent foundrymen, who made first-class iron castings for IBIS Works, Gilbert Gilkes, and grids for street drains in a variety of types, manhole covers and frames for various corporations in the locality, as well as lamp-posts for gas street lamps.

Victrix Engineering Works made several cars, two of which were exhibited at Southport Show in 1901/02. One of the cars, designed by Mr Oliverson, I know was a single cylinder, four-stroke, side valve, water-cooled engine, with its carburettor made from brass castings, which I saw the patterns for when father and I bought some tools from there in later years.

Mr Oliverson was a kind of upper class chap not without funds. One of his failings was that of 'changing his mind', not that all his ideas were impracticable but he seldom allowed any one idea to reach fruition, which the members of his staff found to be most frustrating and which in many cases consisted of practically total redesign of the engine.

This went on for so long that most of his skilled staff decided they had had enough and literally 'walked out'. The Bare brothers, (Walter and George), Walter Killingbeck and Zenas Crabtree all decided to leave. Walter and George were excellent machinists and set up an engineering works on their own account, in premises on Waterside, north of Abbot Hall Recreation Park. Walter Killingbeck went back millwrighting at Wright, Heap & Westwood, in Ann Street. (He was later killed in a motorcycling accident, in the early 1920s - he had an AJS motorcycle). Zenas set up as an engineers' pattern maker in Lound Street. The workshop was over a stable and the ground floor part used to be Bill Mason's stable. (It's still there today but I don't know what it's used for). He started his pattern making business with mainly hand tools.

As already mentioned, there were several woollen mills in and around Kendal at this time. Only Castle Mills on Aynam Road remains and this firm now produces carpets for the domestic market. Prior to the 1939-45 war they produced woollen and worsted cloth for the tailoring trade. During the same war the mill was turned over to the manufacture of cylinder heads for the poppet valve Bristol Pegasus aero engines.

There were in Kendal at that time two major manufacturers in the engineering trade, namely Isaac Braithwaite & Son Engineers Ltd and Gilbert Gilkes (later to become Gilbert Gilkes & Gordon Ltd). We also had in town, Isaac Braithwaite & Son, Drysalters. This was separate from the engineering firm of that name - they dealt with soap and distilled water amongst other things. Both firms of IBIS were in Ann Street, the drysalters near the junction with Longpool (down the lane nearly opposite 8 Ann Street) and the other firm was nearer the Castle Street junction, though not visible from the road, as it was set behind the front row of houses). We also had Henry Rishton (previously mentioned), iron founders and HH Day brass and aluminium founders, all of these named companies required pattern makers for their respective trades. Braithwaite Engineers for laundry machinery, included the American designed Hoffman Press, steam heated and also gas heated irons. These were not domestic tools but were for commercial laundries and also used for the laundries on large ships. They were exported world-wide. Braithwaite Drysalters requirements were much less and therefore infrequent. Gilbert Gilkes, however, were large makers of water turbines, pelton wheels, hydraulic valves etc. At that time my father was doing all the pattern making for IBIS (Issac Braithwaties) in Ann Street works and Gilbert Gilkes at Canal Head.

Gilbert Gilkes at that time was dependant on Rishtons for their iron casting and HH Day for brass and aluminium castings. Much later Gilkes had their own iron foundry, probably about the time Rishtons were closed down by the factory inspectors, who had ordered Mr Rishton to have the leaking roof repaired. The inspector had come back a year later and found the roof to be as it was on his previous visit, whereupon he issued a closure order. Clearly the inspector was not going to have his order disobeyed and Mr Rishton at eighty years of age was not going to be dictated to, especially when the moulders were not complaining. They knew where there was dry working and that is where they did their work. The only losers were the foundry moulders who lost their jobs, in fact some of them never worked again, a very few went to Lancaster. All the grates, manhole covers and other iron work, such as railings, had in future to be bought away from Kendal - so who were the losers? The result was Gilkes (not immediately) built their own foundry and IBIS transferred their business to Lancaster. The work was not to their liking at first, but gradually improved with constant prodding. Some of Rishtons moulders were taken on by the Lancaster firm, which probably was the cause of the step-up in quality.

All the above contributed to Zenas' immediate success in his own business and, before very long, he had to employ two additional pattern makers, Harry Hodgson and Bert Wells. He purchased a wood turning lathe and a new thirty inch Wadkin bandsaw to facilitate the cutting out of the rather intricate shapes for laundry machinery and also for water turbines. He obtained a vertical pillar drilling machine (No. 2 Morse Taper), with rise and fall table. He also made a large grinding machine with a twenty-four inch diameter wheel, five inches in width and running with the lower quarter of wheel diameter running in water to prevent 'drawing the temper' of plane irons and chisels. He later made patterns for double-ended bench grinders that would take ten inch diameter by one and a half inches wide grinding wheels. These grinders had fast and loose pulleys and ran on heavy duty ball races. We had one of these in regular use, right up to 1973 and beyond, after my working days were done at sixty-five.

Amongst other regular users of Lound Pattern Works (as it came known) were Kellow Rock Drill Syndicate, of Penryndeudraeth, North Wales, the Newcastle-upon-Tyne Engineering Company under Hugh Mason, who made the NUT V-twin engined motorcycles until the late 1920s - all the patterns for these engines were made in his works and L S Parker made rotary valve bodies, silencers and castings etc.

By 1912-13 he had become aware of the frequency with which he was having to use the services of W & G Bare for metal turning and screw cutting. Father had electricity installed in his works from the local power station, only two hundred and fifty yards away. Gas lighting was far too dangerous with all the wood shavings and turning lying about, and treadle operating a lathe and a grinder for sharpening chisels and plain irons was just not on. The motor was of course DC (direct current) at that time, made by Cutting Brothers, and was rather unique in the fact that it was variable speed 750 to 1100 rpm, in order to achieve optimum speed for woodworking machinery. In fact, his was one of the first businesses in the town to have had electric power installed, even K Shoes at that time were using steam power, with a boiler house adjacent to the

Patterns made by Lound Pattern Works - NUT 5/6hp V-twin - the first British motorcycle to have air circulation right round the valve ports.

footpath and down a few steps, almost opposite No 1 Beech Villas.

About this time father bought a second-hand SS & SC Lathe (sliding, surfacing and screw-cutting) with seven inch centre height, three feet between centres, non-gap bed and a six inch centre height, two foot six inches between centres, Drummond Lathe. The former of these two lathes was always referred to as the Windermere Lathe - where he bought it. Father had also acquired a very long-gap bed lathe 'Greenwood' from Halifax. This had a four cone headstock and was a full SS & SC Lathe - always referred to as the 'Halifax Lathe'. He had also installed line shafting on plain bearing hangers almost the full length of the works, these had a tendency to run hot and he vowed never to use plain bearings again, so frequent lubrication was required in the 'rafters'. These hangers were later replaced with ball bearings.

Edith, Zenas' wife, had a general store on Lound Street during the first world war, which could only be entered from 6 Beech Villas where they lived. This was quite a large shop and sold everything from gents' suits and ladies' clothing to groceries, confectionery, newspapers and haber-dashery. Made to measure suits were also available - Edith would take the measurements.

Kirkland, Kendal, in the early 1900s (note the houses on the left opposite the tree - this is where the garage was built - nearly twenty years later). Dan Ion's shop shown on the left.

John Marsh Photo Archive

Stricklandgate, Kendal pre 1914-18, with Westmorland Motorcycle Club members gathered outside Neville Abbatt Cycle and Motor Cycle dealer - later this became Craghill & Co's office and showroom. Scott motorcycle and sidecar outside with a small Triumph. NB Harry Rishton's large iron foundry was up the yard where the lady is standing.

Bernard aged three with the motor car (pedal) which his father, Zenas, built. At that time there was no such thing as a pedal car on the market, until many years later. Bernard had his first motoring accident at this tender age, when he lost control coming down the station hill at Oxenholme and ran into a tree at the bottom!

SCHOOLDAYS AND EARLY KENDAL

I was born on 19th October 1908, Bernard Ashworth Crabtree, at 3 Osborne Terrace, Kendal, which is now part of Lound Road. My brother, Malcolm, was born in 1913 and my other brother, Bryan, in 1918. At the age of two and a half I was sent to Miss Simpson's School for toddlers and a young lady called Lizzie Winter, some years my senior, used to take me and saw me safely there and back. Which, when I look back, was very good of her as she lived on the other side of the river at a house opposite the junction of Milnthorpe Road and South Road, so she had to go considerably out of her way to collect me, from No 5 or 6 Beech Villas. I cannot be sure when we first lived at No 5 and when Tim O' Connor, a Police Sergeant, moved into the Old Lound, we moved into No 6 because No 5 only had a cellar kitchen - it may still have!

Miss Simpson's School was towards the far end of the New Road, it was adjacent to the Quaker Chapel and before the stinking tanning yard (long since gone!). My little legs must have been quite tired walking all that distance, keeping up with the longer strides of Lizzie. I had to leave Miss Simpson's when I was five and at this time I was able to read fairly well and to count and do very simple addition and subtraction.

Next I went to a primary school at Kendal Green, where there were three infant grades. Children from five to seven were taken into two classes, one under Miss Allen and the other under Miss Anderson. At five I was of course put into the lower class, where I remained only a couple of weeks, as I appeared to be so far ahead of the other children, due to my reading ability and numeracy. In one year I was fortunate enough to be sent up into the big school, where normally the starting age was seven. This flying start remained with me until I won a Sandes Scholarship for three years at the age of eleven, to the Kendal Grammar School - actually I had reached standard seven by that time.

At that time neither Kirkland School, nor Central School and not even Castle Street were considered to be good enough for mother's first born! The fact that Kendal Green School was the furthest away from where we lived, until my school days were a thing of the past, did not enter into it.

Can you imagine a five year old or even a six year old walking to almost Queen's Road/Green Road, crossing from Beech Villas (Lound

Street) and having to come home for dinner. This I did until I left that school, (except in the most foul of conditions of rain or snow), when I was allowed to take sandwiches and a flask.

Fortunately, in those days 1913-19, there was little motor traffic but, to speed us up, four of us used to take marbles and throw them down the gutter after each other, then run after them, and throw them again; this really kept us on the move and got us home quickly. I don't remember doing this on the return to school quite as enthusiastically!

We came home from school by various routes, the best being of course, by the Main Street and over Nether Bridge into what is now known as Lound Road. Generally we travelled in pairs, Nelson Evans and I who went to Lound Street, and occasionally we were accompanied by Leslie and Douglas Earl and very occasionally by Alma Earl, of course girls were only girls and we didn't mix!

Two of the routes which we took home led us along what is known as 'the waterside' which, in those days, was without fencing or railings from the south side of Lowther Street all the way to the approach path to Nether Bridge. Looking down into the river there were quite a number of stone steps adjacent to the wall - right down to the water's edge and there were mini weirs across the river, probably only about twelve inches high, and these provided ample water for the woollen yarn to be washed in after the fumigation process, which used to kill any life that might still be adhering to the woollen yarn. How they dried at this western side of the river I am unaware - it might have been taken round to the other side of the river and dried in the Miller Field, as I am about to explain.

To relieve the boredom of the long walk from school, we would occasionally go over Miller Bridge, along the footpath on the east side of the road and past the Fire Brigade Station, which was always a splendid sight, until we came to the Castle Mills entrance and the small room adjoining, where stood literally hundreds of circular brass discs with a hole punched near to the top edge and with a number stamped into the centre of the disc hung on the walls. They were early 'clocking on' discs which, when the workers put them into a machine, the time and date was stamped on them. Why the doors into this room were wide open, one leading on to the public footpath and the other into the mill yard, I cannot imagine. It could not happen in the 1990s, all the brass discs would be stolen. So much for morals in the late 20th century.

Proceeding further south we came to the end of the mill buildings proper, to a triangular piece of land before the bridge over the outflow of the channel, which conducted the spent water back into the river.

Upon this piece of land a wooden shed had been built with a flagged floor, at one end of which was a crude hearth on the floor and against the mill wall proper. Inside this building, which measured about fifteen foot by ten foot, were rails running longitudinally the length of the building, these were supported on stout cross beams every yard or so. We eventually discovered the secrets of this building, none of us were more than ten years old - you can't keep kids out! Next time we passed, a whitish smoke was coming through the joints in the boarding and it was pungent, it made one cough. Next time again when we passed the doors were both wide open, the wool was still hanging on its hooks and the fire was out but there were bits of unburnt yellow sulphur in the hearth. We picked up bits of sulphur and of course it went straight into our mouths to test it, we soon spat it out! So, as far as we could see, the yarn which might have been spun at one or other of the mills on the west side of the river must have been washed in the river, carried to the east bank to be dried upon poles which fitted into hooks on the uprights in Miller Field, and there was a field full of such vertical posts to support the poles with the skeins of yarn hung thereon. We did not go back for any more bits of sulphur!

On another way home we came right up Stricklandgate and, passing Blackhall Road, we spied a door to be open which would normally have been closed, so we went in. It was Rainforth Hodgsons brush factory and, apart from the various materials used for making the bristles which ranged from shippon brooms to soft handbrushes, there were kegs of black stuff in which the bristles were later secured, of course we had to have samples of this stuff (pitch, I think) and of course it went into our mouths again - a good job it wasn't arsenic or some other noxious substance, all it did to us was to 'clart' (a Westmorland expression) our teeth up and it was quite a problem to remove!

Facing the top of Finkle Street was a wholesale grocers, Douglas's, and, upon opening the shop, one of the first jobs they did was to put out a wooden box at the north end of their frontage, to be followed by a block of brown rock salt, which must have been one and a half cubic feet in volume. We chipped bits off which we sucked and dogs came and licked it, they also urinated against the box! We were frequently chased away. I believe the rock salt was sold to farmers for 'cattle licks'!

On Natland Road was another mill, again water powered by a mill race from the River Kent, this mill was in operation in my youth and I remember a chap we used to call 'Laughing Johnny' because, apart from towing a huge two-wheeled platform type lorry (I cannot think of a better name) laden with bales of wool to about ten feet high, that was all he did.

This huge platform type structure on two (only) wooden wheels with iron rims, must have been loaded with bales up to a height of ten feet and it was about seven feet wide. The height of the platform upon which the load was carried was between thirty and thirty-six inches high, to the underside of the platform full length and projecting about five feet forward with a transverse wooden peg driven right through the hole provided, in order that Johnny could pull it along. Although the road between Castle Mills and Low Mills was almost level, it was slightly inclined downwards towards Low Mills but, after being processed at Low Mills, it had to go back to Castle Mills for the next process. The weight carried was so great that Johnny was often lifted off his feet, but he hung on because it had a vertical post at the rear which, when it hit the road, bounced the platform up again enabling Johnny to regain his footing. Johnny got lots of taunts from the kids along the route but he could do nothing about it; he simply could not let go of his charge and he had no help whatsoever en route - he had to stick to his charge whichever way he was going. Factory inspectors would not permit such exploitation nowadays and I suppose he would be paid very little for his labour. There were also mills at Sedbergh, ten miles away.

Sometimes, we had to go via Queens Road and down Gillinggate or even by Captain French Lane (which mother did not approve of - she considered it to be rather dangerous in those days). On other occasions, (but never at dinner time - it was too far) we would go via Sandes Avenue and follow the River Kent all the way to Nether Bridge - or even some-times over Miller Bridge and thence via Aynam Road or, yet again, if the canal was frozen over, up Parr Street and via the canal banks. It was upon one such occasion that I fell through the ice almost up to my armpits. I could never quite understand how this happened. I stood on the bank to allow two ladies to get off the bridge, by putting a foot in a hole in the stonework and stepping up on to the bank. When they had both got off, I got on at exactly the same place and went straight through the ice! Naturally I was very wet and very cold and the shortest way home was to cross the ice at the top of Lound Street into Bob Whitwell's field. When I got home mother was horrified and wanted to know every detail, which I told her at length and, when I had finished, she said, "And how did you get home!" To which I replied, "Across the canal to Bob Whitwell's field." She cried, "Have you no more sense than to go on the ice again, what would have happened if you had gone through in the middle?" To which of course there was no answer.

Amongst the thirty pupils in my class, was one whom I remember - her name was Louie Forsyth - as I left that school at age eleven - it must have been before that - I think I was a bit sweet on Louie because I remember chasing her from the school yard, halfway across Kendal Green Fell and when I caught her, I kissed her - my first and only such experience at school. I don't think I ever saw Louie after I left Kendal Green for about twenty-five years!

I didn't learn to swim until some years later at the Grammar School. I must have been about ten, when one day I went via Sandes Avenue on the return home. The river was quite high and we went under Victoria Bridge to be a bit nearer the action. I had a new waterproof coat on that day, and laid it against the bridge wall while we messed about. It was a fine day so then I left and went straight home - mother's first words, "Where's your new coat?" I had to tell her that we had come via Victoria Bridge and I had taken my coat off so as not to get it dirty. "Where is it now?" she said. "Under the bridge," I replied. I had to go straight back and get it, unfortunately someone else had beaten me to it and it had gone and was never seen again.

One other method, we lads (girls I might add, did not get up to such larks!) from the south end of town used to adopt to get home a bit quicker and also to expend less energy, was by running after a horse-drawn cart (you modern ones will not understand this) and get on to the rear axle and get a free ride - the horses pulling the cart at a brisk trot. Sometimes someone shouted, "Whip behind!" Upon which, the driver of the cab took his whip and flicked it back over the top of the cab, and this frequently caught the person getting a free ride in his face, which was quite a painful experience and resulted in jumping off the axle on to the road. Unfortunately it happened to me on one occasion and, partly on account of the speed the cab was going, I landed on my toes and, again due to the speed, I could not regain my footing and run so I was dragged along still holding onto the axle with both hands. At this rate my shoe toe caps would soon be worn through and then I would be in real trouble - the only thing to do was to let go, which I did and landed flat on my belly in the mud. In those days there was mud, real mud and I was plastered from head to foot. When home it had to be the truth I told, one could not invent an excuse for the filthy condition all my front was in and nothing less than a complete change of clothing would do. This took place about 1917-18.

Now, for enlightenment, for those born too late to have memories of the conditions then. Kendal streets and almost every road in the county were made with broken stones rolled and rolled again, until something

KENDAL GRAMMAR SCHOOL.
OPEN-AIR CLASS.

Kendal Grammar School - drawing lesson outside - early 1900s.
John Marsh Photo Archive

like a surface was produced and, to further assist the operation, the roads were watered by lateral sprayers across the back of the water-carts. So much for the roads - tar had not then been introduced. Stand pipes were erected at strategic points to refill these water tanks and one, I remember, was situated at the bottom of Collin Croft. After a heavy rain, the roads were literally awash with mud and they had another horse-drawn device to deal with this. It was a contraption with a steel bar across the back, which could be lowered to road level when required. This bar was fitted with a full row of vertical blades, each about one and half inches wide and which worked up and down on slotted holes. These scraped the road surface and, due to the angle of the bar, all the sludge was scraped into the side of the road and here it was loaded on to a horse and cart, which took it away. Tar did not come until later and when it did, it ran down the camber of the road in rivulets on a hot day and, as lads, we used to pick this up and make balls of tar!

Kendal Grammar School was of course a much larger school, with a very considerable boarding establishment. There were boys there from the Home Counties, Cheshire, Lancashire, the Midlands and even foreign boys from overseas. There was a private swimming bath and a gymnasium with changing and washing facilities, a very large cricket field and a football field adjoining. Games were encouraged and, in addition to the regular half-day holiday, an extra half-day (Tuesday) was given to the boys who were making use of the football, cricket, swimming and gymnasium facilities.

Methods at this school were totally different and I suffered a good deal of bullying. On occasion I was even forced to give my written homework to some other boys - who copied it and returned mine just in time for collection by the various teachers. When mistakes were found in my homework, be it in English, Maths, French or Latin, it was soon spotted by the various class masters and we were all punished for copying, and no-one ever admitted they had taken mine and copied it - mistakes and all!

I was totally disheartened when I learned that my father, who banked with the Midland Bank, had been having a talk to Sam Turner, the manager, who was willing to accept me as a bank employee after a brief test. I was adamant I was having none of this, and point blank refused to go and work in the bank. The immediate question was, "Well, what are you going to do?" To which I replied, "I am going to work for dad." I think this must have rather shocked father, for this was when he began to get ideas of going into the motor trade.

Zenas (not 'Zacharias'!)

1914-18 WAR - KENDAL MUNITIONS GROUP

Meantime, Zenas had been gradually arranging his premises and equipment with a manufacturing capability, as and when circumstances had offered themselves to him. He had the background training of Pickles and Gardners, both manufacturing engineers. When the war became imminent in 1914, he knew that he was unlikely to pass any medical examination, as he had a serious hernia, so with this in mind he continued to increase his manufacturing capability. With the outbreak of war, there was a national call for manufacturing capacity and it was from this call that the Kendal Munitions Group was formed from the following businesses - Atkinson & Griffin, Z Crabtree & Co, H J Croft Ltd, Hadwin Brothers and L S Parker.

A meeting was held and it was decided to write to the Ministry of Supply offering their services. The Ministry duly replied to the secretary of the group, informing them that they were sending an assessor/inspector to inspect the machines the group could muster, in order to assess the type of work to offer them. The assessor was being sent on the London train, stopping at Oxenholme junction in the late morning of a specified day and would the group arrange for a car to meet him. (This is as the story was told to me - I was only six at the time). The group held another hurried meeting to see how they should proceed. The members, I understand, looked at one another non-plussed. H J Croft spoke up confidently saying - "Leave the bugger to me, I'll meet him!" and he did just that!

The inspector was to have inspected whatever machine tools the group could muster - but H J Croft was having none of this and, on meeting the inspector could well have said, "We will have lunch first." H J Croft was quite a seasoned drinker and could hold his liquor well. So, knowing H J Croft, they would have started with a double scotch, which would no doubt have been followed with more - sufficient to say, that by the end of the meal, no doubt the would-be 'inspector of machinery' would not even know where he was or why he was supposed to be there!

He was taken back to Oxenholme Station and placed on the evening through train to Euston, with a home-cured ham wrapped in cardboard, then put in a sack, over his right shoulder and hanging down his left side - with a note attached - "Do not disturb until Euston!" In addition, carefully packed in cardboard boxes and put into the inspector's travelling case, were one dozen fresh eggs, two pounds of farm butter and a pound of sugar. That the man must have perhaps unwillingly handed over his keys to enable this manoeuvre to be carried out, is not in doubt, nor is the fact that he somehow must have managed to reach his home - or more would have been heard about it. As it was - a letter was sent to the department, requesting copies of the drawings of the items it was offering for production to the group!

As I know to be customary in such cases, several drawings would follow for selection. The principal item at that early stage selected for production by the group was the nose caps in brass for the eighteen pounder HE shells (high explosive), which were very urgently required on the battle front in France and Belgium. Another meeting was held by the members of the group and one of the obvious gaps in machine equipment was the total absence of any type of machine capable of thread cutting on a large scale. Hasty enquiries were made of all the principal machine tool manufacturers about the supply and availability of such machines. Every manufacturer was totally overloaded with orders for this kind of machine. The nearest manufacturer to Kendal was Lunds of Crosshills (latterly Landis Lund) near Keighley, Yorkshire. They were telephoned and agreed that they did make machines of the required type, but they were totally inundated with orders, so they were then asked if we could send a representative to see what type of machine they would eventually be able to supply. They agreed to an inspection but stated that in no circumstances would they be able to accept an order, as they were fully committed for years ahead and no amount of importuning would enable the purchase of even one machine. This was understood and agreed.

The Kendal group discussed this fully and it was decided to send Billy Hewitson, a celebrated local engineering draughtsman and my father, Zenas, both of them being acknowledged experts. They went; they sketched; they measured; they made notes of every detail of the machines - dimensions, pitches of worm drives, gear teeth and shaft diameters, lengths etc. They returned to Kendal well satisfied with their day's work.

Billy Hewitson made the working and dimensioned drawings, Zenas then made all the patterns. Rishtons made the iron castings. Gilkes did the heavy machinery and the planing of the beds and ways. W & G Bare did the gear cutting. Parkers and Crofts machined the shafts. Eight complete machines were made - two each for Atkinson & Griffin, two for Z Crabtree, two for H J Croft Ltd and two for Kit Parker, all the machines were identical and made to the same standard. Atkinson and Griffin was located just beyond our garage near to Milnthorpe Road and Crofts was situated where Webster's Yard is now, in Highgate. They had a showroom and a garage, with two different shops in between.

After a longish period, whilst these machines were being made, work on setting up the lathes, etc. and getting the basic machining operation up to a production standard was begun. There was a lot of 'catching up' to be done by the thread millers, which involved very much overtime working on these machines.

In amongst all this activity somehow father was able to do some essential pattern making! For quite long periods a double shift was being operated, but this could not be maintained for very long because a breakdown of any machine could stop the whole production process. Father found it impossible to sustain production at this level without skilled assistance, which simply was not available, and for all trainees to work on regardless was 'not on'! Father had men and women working for him and they even worked night shifts. I remember Mrs Barber and Mrs Scott as being two of the women - I don't know how many we had - and two of the men were Billy Docker and Tommy Scott. Jimmy Barber's wife, I remember, got scalped when her hair became trapped in the machinery!

The nose caps for the eighteen pounder would be supplied either as brass castings or hot brass stampings - I believe both were received. The nose caps, when finished, were approximately 3" in diameter by 1" in thickness and there was a lot of precision cutting and threadwork required. I still have one at home.

All the brass swarf was packed into large sacks and was later re-smelted. About the beginning of 1917 the material was changed from brass forgings to iron castings, with no change to making up details except that the back had now to be machined. This was definitely not welcomed by father as from being a relatively clean operation it became very dirty, although the 'splinters in fingers' problem ceased. The reason they stopped using brass was simple - it was too expensive.

These nose caps each bore the stamped Government acceptance broad arrow. The cast iron forgings came already stamped by the machinist's stamp, in this case 'ZCK', and by what appears to be a forging stamp, either a letter M or W. There was also a ¼" Whitworth tapped hole through to the middle of the internal thread, obviously for a locking

Atkinson & Griffin (their first garage). Highgate, Kendal.

John Marsh Photo Archive

1914-18 War. Wounded soldiers outing by members of Westmorland Motorcycle Club, taken at the 'White Lion', Ambleside. Immediate left of picture - arms folded - Mr A J Miles, next to him standing is Mr H Underhill. Centre of picture arms folded with a cap on is Mr Z Crabtree and next to him on left is L S (Kit) Parker. Note the old Ariel motorcycle on left.

grub screw. I know these were produced by Z Crabtree, Kendal at a very high rate and they were consigned in specially made packing cases, which must have weighed about a ton when packed. The boxes were 30" square by 12" deep, made of 1¼" boards. The lids were of a similar size and construction, well made and bolted, with steel banding to prevent the bottoms falling out with the weight of the contents. All father's cases were stamped and had the letters 'ZCK' stamped prominently on all four sides. They were certainly very heavy, these nose caps weighed 1½ lbs each and the boxes had to be handled by chain blocks. They were sent by rail to Dobbie Forbes, of Larbert, Stirlingshire and William Beardmore of Paisley.

When I was not actually at school, I spent the whole of my spare time drilling the centre half inch diameter hole through the forgings in a six inch centre Drummond lathe - standing on a wooden mineral water box - the drill was a No. 2 Morse Taper in the tail stock. To start with, somebody had to put the nose cap into the lathe, later I could do it myself. I loved it and I felt that I was 'doing my bit'.

The mine sinkers were made from steel bar - about one and half inches in diameter. These were sawn off long bars and threaded at both ends. I think that perhaps they were screwed into the underside of the mine and probably a cast iron weight was screwed on to the bottom end to keep the mine upright in the water and to enable it to float just below the surface of the water, thus enabling the unlucky ship to strike one of the 'horns' with horrific effects to the ship. They were about eighteen inches to two and a half feet long.

The other item entrusted entirely to the Kendal Munitions Group was the manufacture of the whole of the water circulating pumps for the three ton Austin lorry. Austin had only made private cars up to this time but this was a design imposed upon them by the Government Authority, designing fighting vehicles and the like.

The pump body was aluminium and in two halves. It had a steel shaft passing right through, with a brass impeller and with bronze bushes and gland type seals in both halves. The work was split up between the group members, as best suited to their capacity, and capabilities. The Austin three tonner transmission was unusual, to say the least. In place of a single propeller shaft driving a centrally disposed crown wheel and pinion (or worm and wheel drive - as was often the case in those days), it had two open drive shafts going diagonally to the individual rear wheels. These shafts must have had universal joints at both ends. All these parts were brought together and assembled, probably at Crofts Garage in Highgate, Kendal. Many people will never even have heard of an Austin lorry built for the War Office in the First World War - in fact I only ever saw one of these vehicles and I was still quite young; it was owned by a furniture removal firm, Wartons in Kendal. I suppose in the early 1920s it would be replaced by a new vehicle.

Ford 'Model T' as modified by Z Crabtree & Co. Landaulette body specially built by Motor Car Industries, Kilburn, London

C. Fearnsides, King Street, Penrith

AFTER THE FIRST WORLD WAR

At the end of the 1914-18 war, father was left with a lot of machinery and no work for it, so he called in his pal Billy Hewitson again and together they came up with three items to manufacture.

About this time the current type of compulsory road licence disc came into use and he designed and manufactured hundreds of aluminium licence holders. These were all made of substantial aluminium castings in two or three pieces according to type, whether they were a flat back design (two piece) or motorcycle types, eg Druid, Brampton, Triumph etc, or clamping to various makes of front forks and for handlebar fitting - bored to several different standards. These I remember sold for 10/- (50p) each, quite expensive for those days. These aluminium licence holder castings were also made by Robert W Coan and were absolutely trouble free and watertight. These licence holders involved lathe and drilling work and were made to such a high standard that any outer half would fit any back half taken at random, in other words they were not made in selective pairs. These were sold to car and motorcycle dealers over a wide area. However, it was not very long before the market was flooded with licence holders made from very light pressings, with a man hour utilisation of probably only 5% of the fully machined aluminium castings used, so within a couple of years the demand for the 'engineering product' had to be discontinued due to lack of demand.

The Model T Ford cars being then the only cars available in any number, father looked for shortcomings in these cars and also in one ton trucks. First was the very inefficient and fragile design of the rear brake shoes which had flimsy iron castings which frequently broke, especially when the machined half-axle shaft, which ran in Hyatt flexible roller bearings, wore a bit thin and became slack when under conditions of load and rough roads, causing the lower brake shoe to support a large proportion of the weight of the car, plus the shock transmitted to the lower shoe. Father designed a much more substantial shoe with a webbed design and which was lined with ¼" thick die pressed Ferodo brake linings. This was designed and designated 'Crabtree's Patent'. The original Ford shoes were unlined (cast iron shoes to steel drum) and were only adjustable by shortening the effective length of the brake rods.

The Crabtree design incorporated adjustment at the heel of the brake shoes; the first time this had ever been used. Nowadays, it is almost universal in Lockheed and Girling designs. The patent was never renewed and it was only a matter of time before variations of the design came into use. Unfortunately, with very worn half-shafts, shoe breakages still occurred after extended mileages.

In addition to this design he also made replacement radiator caps. These were made from brass castings and were machined and then threaded with the same thread milling machines designed and produced for war production.

With Billy Hewitson, the draughtsman, they designed a two-speed gearbox of such ample proportions that there was never any demand for replacement gears or the massive SKF ball races that were used throughout. These gearboxes ('K' gearboxes) were exactly twelve inches long and bolted directly to the rear-end of the standard Ford epicyclic two-speed and reverse gear. Together these units gave four forward speeds and two reverse speeds. There were two optional sets of ratios available and this had the effect of reducing wear on the engine and reducing petrol consumption of the 23hp Ford engine. It also greatly increased top speed on the road and gave much better performance on hills in the intermediate, between the Ford low and high ratio gear. The gears themselves and gear shafts were made by Barlow & Chidlaw of Manchester and the aluminium gearbox castings were made by Robert W Coan, of 219 Goswell Road, London. One further advantage of the use of these gearboxes was the fact that the chassis was extended by precisely twelve inches, with well-designed extensions which fitted over the rear ends of the standard Ford chassis frame, with a much heavier extension for the Ford one ton lorry. The rear end of the gearbox was supported on a substantial tubular cross member.

The gearboxes, brake shoes and bodies were distributed throughout the length of England. Some firms' names I remember were Peppers at Hanley Garage, near Stoke-on-Trent; Maltbys Motor Works, at Sandgate, in Kent; Tinklers of Penrith; Barton Townley, Lancaster; Quicks of Manchester and County Garage, at Carlisle. All machining operations were carried out at former munitions works, except as stated, for the actual gears.

My father took a Model T Ford chassis down to London and had the first of a long line of landaulette bodies, constructed by the coachbuilding department of Motor Car Industries, Kilburn, London. These bodies were, in most cases, supplied direct to the dealer fitting the gearbox and the chassis extensions. We had no quarrel with that arrangement, which

'K' Gearbox, designed and made at Lound Pattern Works.

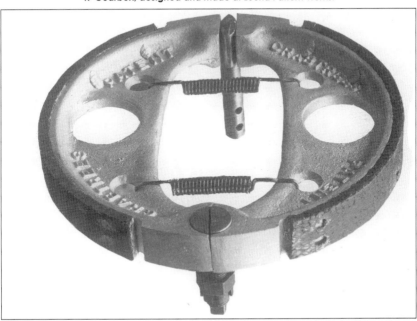

Crabtree's patent 'brake shoes' - lined with ½" thick die pressed Ferodo brake lining - they literally 'never' wore out. Principal later copied by proprietary brake manufacturers. Made by Crabtrees 1920-25.

simplified matters from everyone's point of view.

The car was then taken to the Olympia Motor Show and a good reception was accorded to the design, incorporating four forward speeds and also to the twelve inches longer wheelbase which allowed the rear doors to be full width (with no 12" circle taken from the bottom rear corner), a partition, with glass sliding windows between the driver's compartment and the passenger compartment, and which was also large enough to accommodate two fold down seats built into the partition. The improved braking of the Ferodo die pressed lined shoes, was also much appreciated.

Many Ford chassis were sent to Kendal for the gearbox and brake shoe installation, notably in the London area and the County of Westmorland, where the greater space inside the passenger section was greatly appreciated by the taxi owners. I can only remember helping with one such installation during a school holiday, it was a new Ford one ton chassis for Alf Burrows, the then furniture removal contractor.

Before we go any further, I must mention my father's motor cycles and one or two adventures I had from a very early age. About 1910 my father had an ROC motorcycle, I never had any recollections of this early machine but I do know of the 1914 7/9 Indian sidecar (registration number EC 914) outfit he owned, bought from his motor trade and Westmorland Motor Club friend, L S (Kit) Parker. I remember this machine particularly well because, on my parents' frequent journeys to and from the Hebden Bridge district to visit their parents, I was a passenger with my mother in the sidecar.

The most I remember about the Indian, were the rod operation of the throttle and spark timing controls, which were by a succession of rods with universal joints, where there were changes of direction and of steering movement. It had an impressive barking 'big twin' engine, with overhead inlet and side exhaust valves but its performance was pathetic. On these journeys into Yorkshire it was father's custom to stop at the bottom of Buckhow Brow (to the north of Settle), in order to allow the engine to cool and to have a look at the ebb and flow well. This well had holes in the body of the well almost at the bottom and very occasionally a silver-like air bubble reached right across the bottom from the ingress side to the exit.

One fact of life with the Indian was that it only very rarely, that is if ever, climbed Buckhow Brow without stopping, due to either insufficient engine power or, if the engine was on top form, the clutch would slip - in both cases it was a case of get out and push.

Mr & Mrs Z Crabtree in 1914 7/9 Indian outfit, with Bernard sitting in front outside their house at Beech Villas

`Picture taken of other side of motorcycle on Aynam Road.

Chivalry on the road has gone over the last seventy-odd years. In those days one could hardly stop for a breather without the next vehicle slowing down and in some cases actually stopping to ask, "Are you alright?" or "Need any help?" If you ran out of petrol, they would oblige and help in whatever way they could. Nowadays, they pass at speed and sometimes a bit too close for comfort!

On one occasion, when we got a puncture in the back wheel on the lower slopes of Buckhow Brow whilst returning from Hebden Bridge, mother took me across the road and helped me up the wall into the wood on the eastern side of the road. In that way - 'she would know where I was'. I was playing happily there, collecting a bunch of wild flowers etc - when I received the call, "Come on Bernard, we are going now!" Naturally, I came and when we had been going for about half an hour, I suddenly remembered I had left my money and shouted, "Stop, I have left my money!" I could not be placated until my father said, "Never mind Bernard, you know where you left it. We will stop and get it next time we go to Grandma's." With this, I had to be satisfied and I made jolly sure next time we went we would stop! My parents thought I would be in for a big disappointment - but no, I knew at which precise tree I had left it - made a bee line for it and picked it up. With all the families we called on - at a penny from each, it was a small fortune to me - about a shilling's worth of copper coins!

Tyre changing then was not straight forward, far from it. Without a modern quickly detachable rear wheel, knock out spindle or whatever, a rear wheel puncture in a beaded edge tyre was something to be reckoned with - whether it be at home, in your shed or garage, or when on the road with all your motorcycling clobber on. Well, in those days, one always carried a pump in good working order and a butt ended tube! What's that? Well, imagine an inner tube complete with Woods valve and cut across at a point about 180 degrees from the situation of the valve, then imagine a very slightly smaller diameter of tube, parallel about three inches long and with a cone-shaped end, insert this into one of the cut ends of the tube and solutioned in position. Now go to the other cut end and insert another similar shaped piece, but about twice as long and with a male-shaped cone end, one half of this is cemented into the other cut end of the tube, leaving a projection which exactly fits inside the other end. One simply threads one end round the fork ends and pushes the male end into the female end, puts the tube inside the tyre and the valve through the hole in the rim, refits the tyre, whilst being careful not to pull the tube ends apart when doing so. Inflate the tyre hard and, providing that you have not nipped the tube with the tyre leavers, away you go! Bear in mind, in those days, all tyres were beaded-edged and had to be stretched over the rim. If they were not a tight fit on the rim diameter, it was possible to 'roll' the tyre off the rim when cornering (it happened to me and the tube came out and was chewed up by the chain and sprockets).

In 1916 (how they managed this in the middle of the 1914-18 war I cannot imagine), Kit offered my father a new 3½hp Scott sidecar outfit (registration number EC 1699) which father bought, part exchanging the Indian. The Scott, a parallel twin-cylinder water cooled two-stroke of only half the rated capacity of the Indian, simply flew up Buckhow Brow and never boiled! It had only a two-speed gear but was far better than the Indian with its three-speed gear, both in hill climbing and speed.

Mother's third son, my brother Bryan was born in 1919 and, instead of taking the Scott and sidecar to visit the relatives in Yorkshire in 1920, father bought a new 2½hp single cylinder two-stroke Velocette, with two-speed gear and star change - registration number EC 3000. The 'star' was the shape of the knob which changed the gear, it was on the tank and coupled to the gearbox by a round steel rod. The gear positions were low, neutral and high, and the change was made by twisting the rod to the desired position. This machine was all chain drive but did not have the advantage of having a clutch in the drive, nor a kick starter.

The drill was quite simple, one sat astride the machine, suitably clothed, engaged low gear and paddled the machine forward with the compression release lever lifted, when it reached walking pace, you dropped the compression release leaver and the engine started (it really did). Having accelerated the machine to about 10mph, you then lifted the compression release again, twisted the knob into the 'high' position and adjusted the throttle lever to the desired position and away you went. Mother thought I ought to accompany father, so a cushion was tied on to the quite substantial carrier and I was to put my feet on the footboards, behind father's.

Next, was a serious lecture by father as to 'what to do' and 'what not to do', the most important being the untried Velocette on the terrain we were about to visit and the unknown hill-climbing power of the Velocette. So father explained to me that this was a much less powerful motorcycle than he had ever had before and that he was therefore unable to predict how it would behave on the hills to be encountered. He also explained that without a clutch, he would be unable to restart the machine by paddling uphill. So, he explained the drill he had thought up.

As already stated, it had a two-speed gear and when the steepness of the hill warranted it, he would change from high gear to low. He further explained that if it seemed as though it might be going to stop I should look behind and, if there was no other vehicle there, I should get off and, when he got to the top of the hill, he would wait and pick me up.

He then demonstrated how I was to get off the moving machine, by grasping the outer tubes of the carrier with both hands and gently leaping backwards. Traffic was not a problem in 1920, so we set off. When we got to Cow Brow, seven miles after leaving Kendal, father changed into low gear. I listened carefully as the engine speed slowed and decided it was time for me to leave. I made a perfect landing and ran after the disappearing machine as it rounded the bend and was out of sight and sound. You can imagine my shock and disappointment when I too got round the bend and father was not in sight! I continued to run and eventually broke into tears - I thought he had gone and left me - I continued to run in my heavy clothing.

Father had not missed me, but when he was going down the hill into Kirkby Lonsdale he looked round and spoke - but I was not there. He was, I suppose, just as shocked as I, fearing that I had fallen off! We were soon reconciled and off on our journey, there were no further problems and I never needed to get off again!

Back to business and my father's reasons for entering the motor trade which were two-fold. He was already making and fitting gearboxes for the Model T Ford cars and lorries as already mentioned, which involved the lengthening of the chassis and of course the wheelbase by twelve inches. This, as you will appreciate, involved a considerable amount of work, which the small engineering works could only carry out at the rear of the premises, which involved working in the open and in wet weather it was just about impossible. Added to this, he was making and fitting brake shoes and radiator caps. The other reason was me - it was about the time I would soon be leaving school and I had made it clear that I did not want to work in the bank and had told him that I had wanted to work for him. He could see that I meant what I said and he let the matter drop.

His own personal reason was understandable, when it came out that he was experiencing severe cash flow problems, which I knew nothing about. The man-hours taken to make intricate patterns were very great but unfortunately the reluctance to pay for them, anything like promptly, was very great too and it had become almost necessary to have to plead to get paid. So in one way it let him out of that situation and, if he went into the motor trade, he would have proper facilities for getting the cars under cover for the fitting of gearboxes, brake shoes etc.

KIRKLAND GARAGE
AND STARTING WORK

Father bought the only suitable property he was able to find, at a price he could afford to pay. This involved the purchase of a block of houses which had formed a lodging house complex and, as Mr Murdoch and his wife were now quite old, they agreed to sell the whole block, which consisted of 96, 97, 98, 99 and 100 Kirkland, which ultimately became the largest garage in the town. My father had undertaken a monumental task and I was still at the Grammar School for three years and with much homework to do, so was of no practical help at the time.

The first aim was to clear the front row of the property, starting at the inner edge of the pavement, plus one house built at a right angle to the front property, that was to be phase one. The plans were of course in existence and had been passed. Father made hoarding, largely out of doors for the proportion of the old buildings to be demolished, to protect pedestrians, they were battened together on displaced ceiling joists, with one door through the hoarding for access. Access had to be left also for the carts, yes, horses and carts were used to cart the stone, lime, rubble and later earth, to whichever tip would accept it. Some of the boulders weighed two tons. These were blue stone, they had no grain and could not be broken, so chain blocks had to be used so they could be loaded. Fortunately large works were being undertaken at the far end of the town, which were being levelled (upwards) and several horses and carts were provided by Wilds the haulier.

So the floor was levelled down, the further back from the pavement one went the greater the depth of earth to be moved, in fact as the building stands today, the depth of the garage floor is twenty-two feet lower than the land behind. As one can easily judge, the further one went with the excavating the deeper the spoil to remove. The first phase was to make a garage with a level floor only a couple of inches higher than the pavement at the front and with an interior height of 12' 6" and with a flat built over, which was our home for some time. This was to be a steel-framed building, with only the south front corner of stone, all the remainder including the roof trusses for the flat and for the short length of garage behind were on steel stanchions and steel roof trusses, the

43

Kirkland early 1900s. No 3, Yard 94 Kirkland no longer here (before Z Crabtree & Co)

supplier was Redpath Brown of Glasgow.

Having got so far and with the garage now operational, father decided, unwisely I believe, to gut one of the further properties and bring the machine shop from Lound Street into one of the properties. Just imagine fixing up line-shafting, electric motors, lathes and other machines into these premises, with a floor level almost six feet higher than the floor of the garage and more serious still, in a couple of years to move the whole lot again about another thirty-five feet back. Far better, in my opinion and with hindsight, to have continued to rent the old premises in Lound Street. It wasn't so far away, about one sixth of a mile, if anyone had wanted to use a lathe, after all lathe work is not the main function of a garage. The further the building went back, the taller the properties became and the greater the depth of earth to be removed and transported by horse and cart to start with. Then we acquired a Vulcan light lorry which, although grossly overloaded most of the time, managed to get in an average of thirty loads a day. Horses and carts were soon dispensed with after that. We were chiefly filling up land, as I said, at the other end of town at the auction mart and behind the castle, for a new housing estate at Castle Grove. On Natland Road we filled land opposite Low Mills, where there was low ground in preparation for houses being built and the sand pits, at Gallowbarrow. Indeed any land that needed filling, we did it for them. The Vulcan did a splendid job and the spares service from the factory at Crassons, near Southport, was the quickest I have experienced in my whole life. We expanded the garage in stages as we could afford it.

Differential pinions were the weakness with the Vulcan and, considering that we were tipping on top of newly-tipped earth and were literally bogged down with every load, the differential took a terrific beating. What was more the vehicle had a cone clutch and it was either 'in or out'. The clutch was leather faced and very fierce and even repeated treatment with Collon clutch oil had little effect. In fact, I drove the vehicle for probably thousands of loads, right through Kendal to the Tebay Road and once I had engaged the clutch leaving the garage, generally I never used the clutch again, until I was reversing on to the tip. It had a 'musical' four-speed gearbox - a different tune in every gear - so that it was very easy to judge exactly when to shift the gear and by slowing, in anticipation of arriving behind traffic in front, was no problem; remember we were in the 1920s then with vastly less serious traffic problems than now.

This Vulcan had been taken in part exchange and the previous owner told us the vehicle, when new, had been fitted with a Dorman engine and it had been so much trouble that Vulcan had fitted an engine of their own manufacture under guarantee.

During all this earth removing and expensive expansion in 1927-28, anxious to finish off the job professionally, my father employed the firm of Storey & Sons, plasterers, to give the walls the same quality of finish you would expect to have in your drawing room. This was done to perfection. I ought to mention at this point that the Storey's whole family were the most ardent Salvation Army people in the district. Also, my father had only a few personal friends who ever addressed him by his Christian name, 'Zenas'. Well, when the Storey's bill came, it was simply addressed to 'Zacharias Crabtree, The Garage, Kirkland, Kendal'. Several of these arrived probably at monthly intervals - father took no notice of them and eventually John Storey, the main man, came down and I happened to be there, "Mr Crabtree," he said, "I keep sending you bills and you never pay me, is the job not satisfactory or something?" Father let him have his say and eventually said to Mr Storey, "I keep getting bills addressed to Zacharias Crabtree, when you send me a bill correctly addressed you will be paid." He then said, "You are a Bible man Mr Storey, when you put that matter right, I will pay you." He then quoted Titus chapter 3, verse 13. He got the bill correctly addressed and was paid just as promptly. He never had any problems with being called Zenas to his face and there were some who invariably called him Zenas.

We eventually sited our machine workshop onto an upstairs floor. One half was supported on heavy steel girders, the other half was on earth concreted over, as otherwise we would have been excavating about twelve feet below the boundary wall, which already had a differential of about five feet higher on the far side and not in our favour. Father made a very easy flight of stairs, of ample width and with risers of less than six inches which, compared with ordinary stairs, were very easy. Along came the factory inspector shortly after and ordered that we should fit a hand rail. This was done, made out of one inch bore water pipe 1⅜" outside diameter. On his next visit, he looked at his notes from his previous visit and complimented father for the excellent job he had done. It seems to be a government policy to keep changing their inspectors, upon the principal that 'new brushes sweep clean' and the following year it was a new inspector, who examined the stairs having looked at the notes of his predecessor. He immediately condemned the set-up as unsatisfactory and insisted they were unsafe because anyone could fall under the handrail. Next time he came, he looked at his previous notes and ordered that a lower rail must be fitted forthwith. This time his instruction had to be complied with - on the staircase and on the

Z Crabtree & Co in early days 1923 - the year I started work. Zenas standing on the left with Bernard busy changing a tyre with Tom Chambers standing on the right. Tom became an ambulance driver.

G Wynspeare Herbert, Castle Studio, Kendal.

Zenas Crabtree standing on the main beam. Jack Hutton is on the apex of the steelwork, tightening up all the bolts. Steel was from Thomas Blackburn of Preston - further extensions to the garage in 1937.

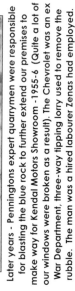

Later years - Penningtons expert quarrymen were responsible for blasting the blue rock to further extend our premises to make way for Kendal Motors Showroom -1955-6 (Quite a lot of our windows were broken as a result). The Chevrolet was an ex War Department, three-way tipping lorry used to remove the rubble. The man was a hired labourer Zenas had employed.

landing at the top but it never was complied with! The inspector was again replaced but the notes of the previous chap cannot have been passed on, and no one ever fell through!

In the meantime, Mr Oliverson had bought a piece of land and built a large house called 'The Hutte' with a badminton court, which had a very high roof with steel trusses and lots of glass, plus gas lighting. The Borough Council later called it just No 30 and today it is a small housing development called Levens Close.

The badminton court was used only for a relatively short time and later for amateur boxing but neither of these lasted very long - in line with Mr Oliverson's previous commitment to car manufacture. Eventually the roof on the badminton court was ruined, caused by children shooting at live birds, which had free access through the large ventilation flaps just below the roof gutters. Windows were consequently broken and slates dislodged as a result. Next door lived Mr and Mrs Bragg, Felicity Kendal's (the actress who took her name from 'Kendal') grandparents.

Over the years Mr Oliverson had tried in vain to make a success of his garage. Firstly, he decided to open a section of his former works (actually only the loading bay and the offices were used) to make it into a garage and petrol station. It failed, I think mainly because he had no employees and only opened for business when he could, therefore his house, gardens and trees, all became a total liability. He took a dealership for the French Salmson light car. The engine of this was of unique design, four-cylinder, water-cooled, overhead valve, with a single push rod, to open both the inlet and the exhaust valves in the same cylinder. I never remember seeing many of these about, although he did run one himself. He also took on the Citroen agency later for a time. This was all unsuccessful and the garage closed and stood empty for a number of years after the first World War. When Mr Oliverson died in his sixties, all his Kendal property, fittings and furnishings were put up for sale by a local auctioneer, Mr I E Kilshaw.

The gas engine that they had in the garage was broken up where it stood - the water jacket was frost cracked, thus rendering it unserviceable, and welding of water jackets was almost unknown in the very early 1920s. The roof of the garage was rusted through with neglect.

At this sale, my father, accompanied by me (aged about fifteen), bought a vertical pedestal drilling machine and large power hacksaw, amongst other equipment, and I remember Chaplows also bought some equipment. (Chaplows at this time had steam-driven threshers and did contracting work from Helsington, where they still are but now in the tarmacadam business).

The garage business went to James Nelson, who bought it for his brother-in-law Billy Dickinson (married to Maggie, James' sister). They managed to get a good business going by employing four workers and eventually became Wolseley agents. James Nelson had the coach works business next door where they repaired, repainted and upholstered car bodies.

However, at the house sale, the reserve price was not reached and it was withdrawn. Some days later, Mr Kilshaw visited my father at his works and said he had seen father at the sale and was he interested? My father, I understand, said, "Yes I am but not at that figure." I don't know what the eventual figure was but father bought the house, badminton court and gardens, which included a tennis court. The house had a large washhouse cellar on the north side, on the south side there were two further cellars, one was called a butler's pantry; the other, quite a large one, had a large stone slab, supported on dwarf brick walls, bang in the middle of the room. It was said to be the wine cellar, there were lots of shelves on the two longer walls. Both of these cellars had windows below ground level, with large pits outside each of them, covered by large rectangular cast iron grilles with parallel cast iron bars - quite safe to walk on, these windows faced south and looked on to the orchard and kitchen garden. One can hardly imagine and, if I had not been involved emptying it, I don't think I could have believed how much rubbish was stored there. We used the Vulcan lorry and took thirty loads of bottles and jars to the tip. It was not possible to walk around the large stone table, bottles were everywhere!

It was the same in the butler's pantry but this was only about one fifth of the size, still one could just squeeze through the door. There were two outside toilets in the yard and one large covered ash pit for refuse, all well-built and slated. There was, on the south wall of the yard, a long covered building, which I can only imagine was for drying clothes and storing logs.

There was no electricity beyond Romney Bridge in those days. Father had the house wired throughout, in anticipation of an electricity supply in the near future, but it did not materialise, so he asked for a quotation for a supply - the price was astronomical, so he would not entertain the idea, and instead bought a Crossley petrol/paraffin engine and a Higgs 2kw DC generator, which was placed in the long room outside - it had snags of course. It started on petrol and, when the small container was running out, you switched over to paraffin, which of course was about

Uncle Frank Greenwood & Aunt Zipp with mother (Mrs Zenas Crabtree) at the drive entrance to the 'Hutte', 30 Natland Road, Kendal. The car is an 'SS Airline'.

half the price of petrol. It was no trouble as a unit. It had to be started by a man in the mornings in winter time, although it was quite easy for a lady to stop it. It also had to be started in the evenings and later in the afternoon in winter. Stopping it was no trouble, one could turn the petrol on to a small reserve which allowed it to run for about ten to fifteen minutes, after shutting the main petrol valve. When it was washing day and on ironing day, someone had to go and start the engine, to provide current for the modern Canadian washing machine and of course, after the drying process, for the electric iron.

So much for the domestic arrangements. After the electricity cable was run as far as Gallowbarrow for the supply to new houses on both sides of the road - electricity became available but father still had a hefty charge for laying the cable up the drive and into the house. Incidentally, the maid saw a rat gnawing at the insulation of the cable, where it came above ground to enter the washhouse (below ground level) above the door, it never came back that we know of.

Between the house and garden, which was professionally laid out with all kinds of tall trees and shrubs, one tree I remember was spliced with two other kinds of tree and the foliage was of three different kinds. There was also a full size tennis lawn, a summer house (octagonal) and, had the garden not been so badly neglected by the Oliversons and later by the Crabtrees (who had no time for gardening!), it would have been a show piece. The principal trees had grown so tall that little light was able to get into the house. One of the mechanics from the garage, Jack Hutton, and I were detailed to go and take twelve feet off the top of all the large trees, thus we did and took the resultant branches to a place near Hawes Bridge, where it filled a rather dangerous gap above the river. It was a number of years I remember before we actually moved into the Hutte to live.

Back to the garage. We had two petrol pumps to begin with, they were not kerbside but had overhead arms - this was to prevent accidents. Later on we had eight then, thirty years later, a dozen pumps altogether. Archie Bryant used to come from Weights and Measures every few months, as well as his assistant, a chap called Winnings. It was an offence to sell short but not too much! In the beginning we sold the Kendal Autocycles, these were fitted with Hobart engines and were ideal for going to work on - easily controlled when the engine was fading on hills, the pedalling gear always meant that you got to the top without dismounting.

Next came Wolf motorcycles, made by the Wulfuna Manufacturing Company in Wolverhampton, they offered a choice of Villiers two-stroke engines or Blackburne four-strokes up to 500cc - all with the typical large outside flywheel - excellent engines.

Then we had Matador orthodox motorcycles made in Preston and fitted with 350cc oil-cooled Bradshaw engines and orthodox in all other respects. After that came Toreador, a similar Bradshaw-engined machine, with one notable difference (which I did not approve of). It had two brake drums on the rear wheel and one at each side but no front brake! A brake can only either slow the wheel turning or stop it altogether; no front brake meant that less than half the braking power (stopping power) was lost. Just look at modern machines with their massive front disc brakes', they know the true effect of front wheel braking!

We also sold 350cc ohv (overhead valve) Blackburne-engined New Gerrards, one of the smoothest running machines I have ever ridden. From time to time we sold OEC machines, fitted with ohv Blackburne engines and 197cc Villiers engines. We were quite successful with scrambles and grass-track racing, with a 197cc OEC we had tuned ourselves. Later in the 1950s, we sold many DMW machines, mostly with 197cc Villiers engines and rear springing, we often had at least a dozen of these machines on hand at any one time.

When I was fourteen, my father allowed me to use a new Wolf Villiers motorcycle to bring in parts from other dealers. On one occasion I was going to Hadwins of Lindale for some Bedford parts and I almost 'ran out of road' on a bad double bend just before Lindale; this of course has been rectified during more recent road improvements. This machine was chain driven and had a three-speed Albion gearbox. Another 'sales machine' I used to ride, was a 350cc horizontally opposed, twin-Douglas, with plain two-speed gearbox and no clutch. This machine had a belt drive. I was also allowed to use a 250cc belt drive, three-speed ratio, two-stroke, ladies' model. This machine had twenty-four inch wheels and the belt pulley on the back wheel was almost as large as the wheel rim. Consequently on a wet day transmission up hill was not reliable. (This machine was a trade-in from Nellie Ellison). I later modified this machine and made it into all chain drive. When riding this machine one day the frame broke. I felt the machine sinking beneath me and I got off and weighed up the situation, looked at the adjacent field walls, selected a suitable stone, then lifted up the sagging machine and wedged the stone on top of the gearbox and under an upper frame tube, then calmly rode the machine back the mile or two to the garage, where the necessary work was done to repair it and transform the machine into a gent's model. I also had ridden a Triumph Ricardo 490cc, ohv, four-valve, three-speed, all-chain drive, belonging to Norvel Roberts.

When I left school in 1922, we broke up at 11am and I went straight to work the same afternoon and immediately got a job helping Harold Metcalf, who had come to work for us from Thornton Motor Engineering Company of Bradford, where he had been foreman in their workshop. This was probably one of the most advanced garages in the West Riding of Yorkshire. The main attraction to him to come to Kendal was not to work in a then small time garage, but so that he could be near his lady friend - one Lydia Wilkinson - who lived only three or four doors away. Harold was father's only mechanic at that time.

The first car I had dealings with that first afternoon was a Stoneleigh, belonging to a Mr Woollat. It was a horizontally opposed, twin cylinder, air-cooled car which, judging by the size of its cylinders, must have been at least 10hp, obviously larger than the Rover 8 which was to follow a few years later. Harold soon sorted it out. I cranked the engine whilst he checked the contact breaker and the timing. Harold got the car going quite soon and Len Woollat was on his way back to St Albans, from whence his parents had come to collect him. Len was in the same form as me at Kendal Grammar School, the school which I had left that day!

That was the beginning and I was thrilled to have got a start at work that very day. Harold was a clever mechanic and I learnt a great deal from him, he had one or two faults (haven't we all!) He was a bit short-tempered and liked a drink.

Undoubtedly, Harold was highly skilled and I rapidly found out that there was no such thing as 'near enough,' it was always 'right or wrong'. A principle I adopted and one which coincided with my father's precise methods, applied to his engineers pattern making and also later to his acquired skills in engineering. I succumbed to the odd slap across the ear and the occasional kick up the backside, when a mistake was made or an instruction was not carried out precisely. It did not matter that I was the boss's son.

Charlie Ralph, was one of the butchers who sold meat round the country areas in the days before decent 'bus services and whilst cars were still few and far between. In Kendal alone there were the following butchers' vans I can remember - J T Long in Stricklandgate, Bob (R) Brennand (Kirkland in those days), later he had a larger shop next to the Westmorland Gazette Office in Kendal, he had finished his meat round by now - 'buses were everywhere. Gilbert Brennand in Allhallows Lane, the Co-Operative Society had several shops in Highgate, Kirkland and Wildman Street. In addition to all these, there was Haytons of Staveley,

Malcolm, aged seven on the 247cc Radco after modifications. Note the ridiculously low position of the seat and small amount of ground clearance under the three-speed hand change Burman gearbox. Originally a ladies open frame model owned by Nellie Ellison. Ford car on the right and to the left Broomby's of Sandside, Sawmill truck.

Netherfield Co-Operative Society Limited (our local Co-Op).

who used to have rounds in the town. So we were well catered for in Kendal by the butchers.

Kendal also had three different roundsmen who came into Kendal selling fish, all from the Flookburgh district. Flukes, shrimps, cod and occasionally crabs were available. Fish from these sellers was generally less expensive than from shops in the town and they were eager to sell out and get back to Flookburgh for the next catch, according to the tides.

Generally, Harold Metcalf was my greatest asset as instructor and, considering we are still talking 1923, it was still early in my career. As mentioned, Charlie Ralph the butcher was a regular customer who ran a Model T Ford van when delivering meat, which was fitted with a twelve cylinder, converted ex-aeroplane magneto. Unfortunately the van had a leaking radiator which, when he stopped to deliver his meat, occasioned him to cover the magneto with a piece of waterproof cloth, to prevent water entering the magneto. Occasionally he forgot to remove the cloth before starting the engine, which caused the magneto driving chain to come off its sprockets. On the day in question, he had stopped at the Punch Bowl Inn, Barrows Green, to serve the landlord with his meat requirements. He stayed chatting for a few minutes then ran out to his van and tried to start the engine! Off came the magneto chain. He went back into the pub and spoke to the landlord and asked if he could use the telephone and explained how the magneto chain came off. He made the call and my father sent me out on a motorcycle to deal with it. He put the 'phone down and said to the landlord that a fifteen year old lad was coming out on a motorcycle to put the chain on and re-time the magneto. The landlord laughed and said he didn't believe him but Charlie said it was right. The landlord bet him half-a-crown the lad couldn't do it, Charlie took him on and won his bet - no problem!

About 1924, Norvel Roberts had ordered a sidecar from Pride and Clarke, London. This came by passenger train and was delivered to us by Edwin Storey, who drove a horse-drawn large parcel van for the Railway Company. Norvel had told us he had asked for it to be delivered to us, and he came in to see it on the day it arrived and asked if we would fit it to his Triumph. Father said we would and when he had gone he then said to me, "Do you think you can do that, Bernard?" I had never done this before, so he gave me a few points. I had to prop the motorcycle up on a level floor under the footrests and make sure it was 'plumb'. Then set up the sidecar wheel slightly ahead of the motorcycle back wheel. In this position, I had to make all the sidecar connections to the motorcycle frame. Remembering that the motorcycle should on no account lean towards the sidecar, and making sure that a straight long board touched the sidecar wheel rim at front and rear and about six inches above the floor, and with a similar straight board against both wheels of the motorcycle, about the same height above the floor, to adjust the fitting until the boards were parallel. Having checked these points several times, I went to father for approval or otherwise of my efforts. He was very pleased and no further adjustment was required. He did however check the tightness of all the bolts at each point of attachment to the machine. His next remark was a bit of a shock. He said, "Mr Roberts wants an overall waterproof detachable apron to cover the whole sidecar aperture, with generous overlap all the way round and to be secured with turnbuckles at about six inch intervals. Do you think you can ride the outfit down to James Nelson's coachworks, next to Victrix?" I had never ridden a sidecar outfit before and was very apprehensive.

I promptly agreed, to which he retorted, "I know you have ridden many kinds of motorcycles but they have all been solo, you must take it very slowly or the sidecar wheel will lift and leave you with little control." I set off at quite a moderate pace because Nether Bridge, with its ninety degree left-hand turn on to the bridge, was only about one hundred yards distant. All went well for the hundred yards but as soon as I turned the handlebars to the left - up came the sidecar wheel - it was a very light sidecar and probably very cheap mail order from London. Every time I tried to turn left to regain the proper side of the road, up came the sidecar and this went on the full length of the 'K' Shoe works, past the entrance to the Old Lound, after which there was a gap where cattle used to be brought by John Nelson (James' brother) to be watered. I somehow contrived to get the front wheel inclined to the right due, I believe, to the increasing adverse camber; whereupon I thought enough is enough, braked to a standstill, stopped the engine and pushed the outfit the last fifty yards across the road and into James Nelson's body shop. I don't think I ever told dad of my near disastrous short journey with the sidecar outfit.

Not long after this, father sold a new 498cc, two-speed Scott and a new Watsonian sidecar. It was again my lot to fit the sidecar to the machine. The motorcycle came by passenger train to Kendal Station and it fell to me again to collect it. Taking a half gallon can of petrol with me, I arrived at the station, removed the protective covering and put the petrol in the tank. The Scott machines were years ahead in many respects; the frame itself was very substantial and of the open frame type suitable for skirts or trousers. The engine was an inclined, twin cylinder, water cooled, two-stroke cycle. The drive was all chain - even the two speeds were obtained by two separate chains and sprockets to the countershaft. Engaging low gear was simply done by pressing the heel down on a pivoted lever; top gear was engaged by pressing the forward part of the pivoted lever down, both engagements were smooth with the built-in clutches. The petrol tank was oval and cylindrical, attached to the down tube supporting the saddle, the oil reservoir filler was just under the nose of the saddle and the main frame-member contained the oil supply (no separate tank). The kick start was operated by the left instep on a crank just ahead of the rear wheel spindle, on the offside of the machine.

My father, as I have already mentioned, had owned a 1916 model (registered number EC 1699) Scott and I knew my way around it by long association, although I was of course far too young to have ridden one at that time. Getting the machine going and back to the garage was no problem, as I already knew the layout of all the controls. The sidecar was ordered direct from the makers, Watsonian, and it was totally superior to the Pride and Clarke unit, which was a cut price affair, and the Watsonian was considerably heavier, but with the Scott's power it presented no problem. The machine was purchased by a Miss Nellie Ellison, later a farm worker at Selside. She handed in a 250cc ladies' model Radco in part exchange. The Radco (as mentioned earlier) I used for picking up spare parts from garages. I went to her wedding from Dry How, Selside. She was a very jolly and friendly lady, who took to riding the Scott and sidecar 'like a duck takes to water'!

Harold was away one day - he had gone over to Bradford for the weekend. A Model T Ford was towed in with all the wiring burnt out. Fords had their own wiring system, very complicated to a beginner, with its four separate trembler coils on the bulkhead, a commutator at the nose of the camshaft and the whole lot in a wiring loom that had been well and truly burnt out. My previous experience was nil, yet my father expected me to get it all put right. My father was a top class pattern maker and engineer but he was no motor mechanic or electrician and as I, at that time, was the only person available, I just had to try but, when you come across a certain wiring loom with rubber insulation burnt out, there is no clue which wires go where?

After a couple of hours getting nowhere, I was quite fed up and it is not a pretty sight to see a fifteen year old hopeful young man crying, and that is just what I did. I stuck at it the whole day and finally began to see the light. When I got all five lamps, the electric horn and all the ignition system operating satisfactorily, I felt as though I had really done something. Since then I have had extensive instruction at Edison Swan Electric Co, Ponders End, Middlesex and at Joseph Lucas Ltd, Great Hampton Street and at Great King Street, Birmingham, all of which opened up new horizons to me in this field.

When I was fifteen and busy working in the garage, black as a sweep - I know I was this age because I had a driver's licence for a motorcycle, but I could not get one for a car until I was sixteen. Harry Forsyth (Louie's father - the girl I had been sweet on at Kendal Green School) was employed by Ridges Pure Boiled Sweets manufacturers in Yorkshire, as driver/salesman. The van he was driving was a 10 cwt capacity Model T Ford. I knew Harry as a customer, who bought fuel and oil from the garage and occasionally had minor repairs done. This time, he came on foot to the garage as he had broken down at Tebay. He said, the rear nearside axle-shaft had broken off and with it the rear wheel, near to Lune Railway Bridge at Tebay, on a short very steep hill (1 in 4 gradient) and was very close to the wall. By the time he arrived, it would be between 8.30-9pm but still daylight. He told my father and me in detail of the incident, he had perforce to leave the van where it was, still partly loaded and it was not lockable.

Father said to me, "Do you think you can deal with this, Bernard?" I said, "Yes!"

He then said "Well get together everything you will need and get away first thing in the morning. Harry will drive you there with all your tackle." I had already had experience of this job and, at that time, we had no other mechanic available for some reason or another.

Although we were not Ford dealers, we were getting lots of Ford work and I loaded up our Landaulette with every conceivable part that could possibly be required, including tools, jacks, empty oil drums, packing, blocks of wood, oil, grease, paraffin, washing off tray and brushes.

We got away in good time and we were at the scene by 9.45am next day. It was certainly near the wall - too near, but we could do nothing about that - trolley jacks had not been invented at that time. Anyone with Model T experience will know what a formidable job I had under-taken; first, it had to be lifted and made safe, quite high above the road, supported on oil drums and blocks of wood. The whole axle and torque tube assembly had to be removed and this involved the disconnecting of the very awkward transverse rear spring and getting the blocks in and out was always a problem.

The torque tube and propeller shaft had to be removed, as did the offside rear wheel and hub. The rear axle had to be split into its two

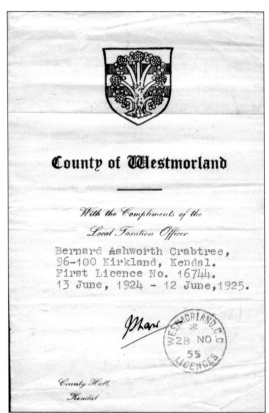

Bernard's first car licence - you did not have to take a test in those days!

D.L.2 **K 9809**

WESTMORLAND COUNTY COUNCIL
ROAD TRAFFIC ACTS, 1930 to 1947:

DRIVING LICENCE

Bernard Ashworth
Crabtree
of Meadbeck
Dowdales
Kendal

is hereby licensed to drive MOTOR
VEHICLES of all Groups from
....D...... 19... until
....D.... 19... inclusive

CLERK TO COUNTY COUNCIL,
Fee of   Motor Taxation Dept.,
5/-   County Hall,
received.   Kendal
Usual Signature of Licensee :

Bernard A. Crabtree.

D.L.2 **744**

WESTMORLAND COUNTY COUNCIL
ROAD TRAFFIC ACTS, 1930 to 1956:

DRIVING LICENCE

Bernard Ashworth
Crabtree
of Moorfields
Crosslane
Kendal.

is hereby licensed to drive MOTOR
VEHICLES of all Groups from
15 January 1958
until 1 January 1961.
inclusive.

Fee of   THE LOCAL TAXATION OFFICER,
15/-   County Hall,
received.   Kendal.
Usual Signature of Licensee :

Bernard A. Crabtree

Later issued with a driving licence book and licence renewed annually and signed

60

halves in the centre, which then exposed the crown wheel, pinion, differential etc. Next the differential had to be split and the broken half-shaft drawn through. Then the sun wheel had to be removed from the half-shaft, this alone involved driving the sun wheel further on the shaft, then removing two semi-circular clips from an annular groove in the shaft. Having done this, the pinion was then free to be driven off the shaft. The new shaft thus prepared, was made ready and it was then assembled in a differential case.

At this juncture Harry said, "We will walk up the road now to the Junction Hotel in Tebay," where we had a good hot luncheon - my first venture of this kind in the whole of my subsequent fifty years in the motor trade - quite an adventure.

When we returned, nothing had been touched, nor had any sweets been stolen. Considering the sweets had been left overnight and again when we had gone for lunch, I wonder how we would have fared nowadays!

We now reassembled the axle and torque tube assembly and refitted the whole unit into the chassis - the rear spring connection was always difficult on the Model T but we managed.

When it was completed the brakes were adjusted, oil was put in the rear axle and the vehicle was generally cleaned up where we had been working. All the clobber was put back into the Landaulette, when Harry said, "How are we going to manage? I can't drive both vehicles back to Kendal!" I said, "Don't worry Harry, take your van back to our garage and leave it there, get a bus back to the last houses on Spital level and I will be there with the Landaulette and contents." He then asked if I could manage. I said, "Don't worry, how do you think I have managed so far? I just don't want to be picked up by the Police. I am known to most of them and there are the odd ones who would like to book me!"

On my 16th birthday I was one of the first in the Licence Office, in Fleece Inn Yard, Kendal, to get my 'car licence'. I never passed any car test but I did some years later have to pass a HGV test, again no problem.

We maintained a Ford Model T Landaulette which we used as a 'private hire car' and it was of course fitted with our 'K' gearbox and adjustable brake shoes. It was also fitted with a Zenith updraught carburettor (the carburettor on all Model T Fords was, of necessity, fitted very low on the offside of the engine, in order to provide a flow by gravity from the under seat situation of the long cylindrical petrol tank). Even this did not provide a satisfactory fuel flow to the carburettor up a one in four gradient (eg Beast Banks in Kendal town centre and the

Greyhound hill leaving Kendal, on the shortest route to Sedbergh), unless the fuel tank was full. Many are the times that such cars with half full tanks have had to reverse up steep hills in order to obtain a gravity supply to the carburettor, otherwise it could mean a long walk to buy extra petrol. In those days two gallon petrol cans were in regular use and supply. One did not often make a practice of running with a low fuel level - unless the run was to be in relatively flat terrain.

Tom Hackett who lived at Castle Garth, was works manager at Mealbank Mill (water powered), and Mr Applegate owned the mill and lived at Stone Cross. Mr Applegate telephoned asking if we could send a mechanic as he was unable to start his car, a Lorraine Dietrich (French car). I was sent on my then Model E 500cc Ariel motorcycle and was probably travelling about 35mph along Milnthorpe Road towards Stone Cross, when a Clyno two-seater car, with the hood down, cut off the corner completely coming out of Milnthorpe Road and ran into the rear end of my motorcycle. The point of impact was fifteen inches behind my left leg (fortunately behind) or my leg would have been smashed to bits. I went flying across the road, somersaulting several times and finished up on the footpath at the other side of the road. I had no broken bones but I ached all over for the next two or three weeks. The driver never saw me, nor I him. The wall on that corner used to be considerably higher than it is now. The driver had an artificial leg and obviously did not have proper control. My machine at that time was insured third party fire and theft, but they did pursue the owner and succeeded in getting £28 from him, which figure was exactly what I had to pay for the replacement parts and for which I had to produce bills. Nothing was paid for the labour charges nor for my inability to work for the next two weeks. How Mr Applegate went on, when I did not arrive at his house, I never discovered.

Tom Hackett, in addition to being works manager, was also responsible for the making of the dyes to the required shades. I learnt later from Tom, whom I got to know after I was married, that it was a very busy mill. He said they made exclusive patterns and high quality cloths for the top Paris couturiers and their traveller regularly took patterns and samples abroad. Much of this cloth was exclusive and, when a particular order was fulfilled, no more of that particular cloth was ever to be made. That was the condition upon which the order was placed. On one occasion (only) that I am aware of, Tom found a remnant of one of these cloths, which was quite literally two cloths in one. One side was a plain grey, whilst the other side had a very large off-white check pattern. From this remnant my wife and myself both had greatcoats made, which

Z Crabtree & Co 1928 and shows the flat above the garage.

Atkinson & Pollitt (Kendal Photographers)

were reversible, they could be worn inside out and were done so on occasion.

The Model T car was in decline due to the host of new cars coming on to the market, plus the number of American cars being imported. Amongst the Americans were: Chevrolet, Buick, Maxwell, Essex, Overland and all at sensible prices. There were also many British makes coming forward, chief of which at that time were Morris cars, fitted with Hotchkiss engines, made under licence from Hotchkiss of Paris. There were also Singer, Swift, Riley, Lea Francis, Cluley, Humber, Calcott, Rover from Coventry factories, plus Austin, Rhode, Daimler, BSA and Wolseley, to name but a few from Birmingham. In fact there were many other makes most notably from the Crabtree angle - Clyno of Wolverhampton, for which my father took on the dealership.

The first of these to be delivered had a 10.8hp Coventry Climax engine, a three-speed and reverse gearbox and four full width brake shoes in each drum, in a very ingenious design. The only trouble we ever had with Clyno were second gear teeth, which wore quite soon at about twenty thousand miles and the fabric flexible driveshaft couplings between the floating gearbox and the flywheel clutch did not last very long (about 10,000 miles). They were reliable, go anywhere cars and economically priced. They later introduced 13hp and 9hp models and I believe over extended their credit in trying to keep up with the Morris Cowley, Morris Oxford and other models in that range. The brakes fitted to the redesigned Clyno models (after they departed from ½ elliptic brake shoes to semi-elliptic) were the best in the small car business at that time (1925).

The large picture of our garage which I date as 1928 for the following reasons - Ethyl petrol was introduced by 'Pratts' later known as Esso, it was about mid 1927. This was followed months later by BP, which was tinted blue, whereas Pratts Ethyl was tinted red. It was many months before we could obtain BP Ethyl because of opposition by a competitor, so it must have been 1928 before we could possibly have got supplies of BP Ethyl, plus a globe, which had to come from BP themselves. Also, it was early 1929 when we got the Armstrong Siddeley franchise. The sliding screen which also folded was made for us specially by 'Stone's' of Ulverston. We could actually just get one Armstrong Siddeley short 20hp saloon and one 12hp saloon into the very small showroom - but it was a work of art manhandling the cars into position.

Crabtree's later took on Armstrong Siddeley and later Hillman and MG cars in the 1930s. In later years as a result of this, Crabtree's Garage, in Kirkland, had to be split into two businesses - Z Crabtree and

Company and an offshoot company (1956) - Kendal Motors Limited. Z Crabtree Company had to make an internal showroom where the office had been and they were agents for the Rootes Group - Hillman, Humber, Sunbeam, Singer and Commer. Their cars had to be displayed in a separate showroom away from their other business, which was as agents for MG and Morris Commercial. These continued right up until I retired in October 1973.

The Armstrong Siddeley make of car has very old roots in the history of British car manufacture even before Sir John Siddeley came into the company and much later his son, Cyril Siddeley. Originally, there had been Armstrong Whitworth cars, Stoneleigh, Armstrong Siddeley 14hp and 18hp models, all good reliable cars but all with very noisy three-speed gearboxes without synchromesh. I think the six cylinder, side valve Armstrong Siddeley would be the first with a three-speed, synchro-mesh gearbox but by the time this model was introduced in 1928-29, the drift was already towards the almost silent 'pre-selector gearbox' (self-changing). This new gearbox had been developed in a closed-off working area inside the Armstrong Siddeley factory at Parkside in Coventry, during the years 1920-28 by Major Wilson, who in fact termed it the pre-selector gearbox. This was because the driver simply selected the gear he was going to use next manually on the steering wheel and the gear did not in fact change until the clutch pedal was sharply depressed, the change was silent and instantaneous. The gearbox was barely audible under any conditions. One could in fact change from a forward gear to reverse without difficulty but this was not recommended on account of the immense strain it put on the whole transmission system - quite apart from the actual load on the gearbox. This was a tremendous advance in gearbox design.

Self-changing gearboxes were later used by other car makes: Riley, MG, Lanchester, BSA and possibly others. The principles of the Wilson gearbox were later used in the Borg Warner and other automatic gear-boxes worldwide. The Borg Warner uses a similar system on drums and contracting bands but it changes by itself when certain preconditions are encountered, eg engine speed, load on the car and other conditions being exerted upon the engine and road speed.

Most of the post war production of Armstrong Siddeley were fitted with self-changing gears, but if a client wanted a synchromesh four-speed gearbox, they were available from Humber Ltd, whose gearbox was easily adapted to the Armstrong Siddeley and there was no extra cost involved.

Just before the war they introduced a Sixteen horsepower, six cylinder model, with much softer springing than hitherto, I took one up to Langdale about twenty miles northwest of Kendal, the car was nice to drive and easy to handle but by the time I had got there and given the demonstration run and then back to Kendal I felt nauseated, in other words sea sick or car sick. Although our client already had an Armstrong Siddeley he would not countenance buying one of these and nor would I! I don't think I ever saw another Armstrong Siddeley Sixteen since that day but the war was on top of us soon after that and, as the factory was utterly destroyed, probably everything connected with the Sixteen would have been destroyed also. I don't think it would have been a success without a total re-design of the suspension system.

During the whole of the time we were agents for Armstrong Siddeley from the late 1920s, on only one occasion did we get a call for help - this was from Miss Corbett who lived at Skinburness, who had a 12hp, six cylinder, self-changer. Somehow, I think that perhaps she had not selected the gear precisely and the clutch pedal had come right up beyond its normal travel and she could not push it down again. Laura (who later became my wife) and I went to Skinburness in a Singer 9 car, on which we had just finished a rebore job. We thought it was a good opportunity to give the rebored engine a run and at the same time give Laura a run out - she did not get many at that time and she knew Miss Corbett. I checked all the external linkage, etc, and found that with one almighty push on the clutch pedal, with neutral selected, it was OK.

The next time Mr Chorlton, the regional representative, came round my father brought this occurrence to his notice and suggested that a member of our staff should go down to Coventry to be instructed on how to deal with any problems. After discussion, it was decided it was not practical for them to travel to Leeds, which was the nearest garage dealing with such cases. I was requested to go to Coventry for two weeks' instruction. As it happened, I was put on the assembly line for a batch of self-changing gearboxes for the Daimler Company, which happened to be going through at that time. They were unmistakenly for Daimler, because the gearboxes for Daimler were rigidly attached to the power unit, whilst those for all the Armstrong Siddeley models had a 'floating' gearbox, rigidly attached to the torque tube and it floated slightly on a spherical mounting attached to the central frame cross-member. This difference meant that the actual gearbox shell for the Armstrong Siddeley and for the Daimler were totally different outwardly, but the internals were identical as were all the internal machinery dimensions - in other words the internals were interchange-able.

We took up the Rootes agency in 1933-34. They had introduced one or two very useful models - the Minx and the Wizard, the Minx being 10hp and the Wizard came with alternate engine sizes 15hp and 20hp, six cylinder models. All these were thoroughly satisfactory motor cars and performed well, the engines in particular having a very long life. The only weakness with the Minx was the liability of the rear axle shafts to shear at the hub end; but this was not only common to the Minx, the Morris Cowley and Oxford models had the same problem, in fact, although we were not Morris agents, we were buying standard quality axle-shafts by the dozen and we were also buying a super shaft at a premium price for those owners, who were tired of breaking down with a broken half-shaft. Hillman also produced a Vortic model, a straight eight cylinder car, but I don't think it was a huge success - I only ever saw one on the road.

We were a pretty broad-minded garage and would supply any make or model of car the customer fancied. Here is a list of such cars, trucks and motorcycles that I know we supplied from time to time: AC, Allard, Alfa Romeo, Alvis, Berliet, Bayless Thomas, Singer, Durant, Hillman, Humber, Sunbeam and Sunbeam Talbot, Ford, HRG, Rolls Royce, Riley, Salmson, Healey, Renault, Riley, Swift, Rhode, Vulcan, Talbot, Cubitt, Bean, Lea Francis, Dennis, HE, Vauxhall, BAC, Jaguar, Standard, Datsun and Aston Martin. There have been very many manufacturers who have simply gone out of business due to the competition.

The first motorcycle I bought was a 350cc, ohv, New Gerrard, with a Blackburne engine, three-speed Burman gearbox and of course all chain drive with a top speed of about 67 mph. One pal, Bill Clow, who had a 344 HRD with a twin-port, ohv, JAP engine, always claimed it to be better than mine and he tried to convince me how much better JAP engines were than Blackburne's. Of course we never agreed; the fact was he could never leave me behind and in fact Bill's machine was less stable. He frequently criticised the New Gerrard because it had no steering damper, the fact was that his machine needed a damper. I remember we used to go down to Lancaster quite often and between Beaumont Canal Bridge leaving Lancaster to Slyne, there was a row of manhole covers, perhaps sixty or seventy yards apart. Bill could never ride over these without his damper being screwed down - it immediately got into a serious wobble, whereas my machine never tremored, in fact it could be ridden over 'hands off!'

On another occasion when I was going for a ride with Tom Chaplow and Bill Gray, I realised my back tyre was soft as it was rolling a bit on the corners and they were ahead of me so I tried to catch them up.

Armstrong Siddeley, Short 20 - property of Mr G E Gregson, Low Hackett, Little Langdale - 1929

1926/27 New Gerrard 350cc Blackburne - one of the nicest bikes Bernard had ever ridden.

Unfortunately my back beaded-edge tyre came right off the rim, the tube was chewed to bits in the back chain, the bike dived across the road, ran up a heap of road chippings about four feet high and down the otherside. I was still in the saddle and, although scared, was still right end up and in control!

Back in 1927, Tom Chaplow on his 500cc AJS, Bill Gray on his 500cc BSA Sloper and I on my Blackburne were going to Sedbergh. Unbeknown to them, Esso had given my father a two gallon can of a new petrol - Essol Ethyl - to test and father never went anywhere really, so he gave this to me saying, "Bernard, you had better try this in your motorbike and let me know what you think of it!"

Off we went and as we got to the main hill (Roan Edge), going over to Sedbergh, I was able to keep up with both of them and even go ahead. Of course they wanted to know what I had done to the bike, so I said, "Nothing, other than filling the tank from a new petrol in one of our pumps and it seems to be pretty good!" The performance of the bike also surprised me.

With this machine, I first became interested in trials riding and the local Westmorland Motor Club, of which my father had been a member for very many years, but which was currently in abeyance.

Laura in 1928.

LAURA

It was only a few weeks after I had got my motorcycle, the OEC Blackburne (which incidentally was one of the earliest Blackburne engines with inside flywheels) that I met Laura, outside her front garden gate, at 'Moorfields', Oxenholme, with her pal, Kathleen Raffles (the then Stationmaster's daughter).

Shortly after that, Laura's mother said to her, "There is a young man I have seen flying past here on his motorbike, he can't go very far, because he is back again in a few minutes. I wonder who he is and what he comes up here for?" Laura quickly answered, "Oh, he comes up here to see me!" She said, "See you? Who is it?" Laura said, "Oh, it's Bernard Crabtree, they have a garage in Kendal." I think Mrs Pinch must have been speechless! That was all I heard at that time. I was asked to go and meet her parents, which was something I put off for as long as possible. I was extremely shy at that age as I would be just twenty and I had given up smoking permanently - in order to be able to afford the OEC. In fact it was quite some time before I plucked up the courage for an introduction to her parents.

We got on like a house on fire and we did much motorcycling together, as a road bike the OEC was marvellous, so much so that on one occasion, returning from Patterdale and Aira Force, we ascended that side of Kirkstone Pass in top gear, the speedo never indicating less than 55mph and its road holding was magnificent. In October I sold it to a pal and took his model 'E' 500cc Ariel in part exchange - it could not live up to the OEC on the road with a top speed of 72mph against the 100mph of the OEC - that was the reason he wanted it. Before I released it to him, I de-tuned the engine so seventy was its top speed, he railed against this but I told him I had done it for his own good - he liked his drink and I was teetotaller! He found a buyer for it, but before he came for it (he lived in Ulverston) he asked me to restore it to its original form - or he would not buy it, which of course I did and put it back to how it was when I had it. My friend was not too pleased but accepted my reason for so doing.

Laura and I went all over the Lake District on that bike, she was a marvellous pillion passenger, she sat there feet on the footrests, hands in pockets and just let herself go with the banking of the machine, really one could not tell there was a passenger aboard. I bought her a ladies leather coat and leggings and she was fine. When the weather was good and I was not stuck on a job, I used to go on the bike to Jack Robinson's dental surgery in Highgate, where Laura worked, pick her up and take her to Oxenholme for her lunch and she usually returned to work on the 'bus. If I wasn't there before the 'bus left for Oxenholme, she knew I was stuck on a job. Going on the bike gave her a full fifteen minutes extra time at home.

Laura and I went on regular dates from April to December, when I took her to the Westmorland Motor Club Annual Dinner at the County Hotel, Kendal. Not long after that, she began to put pressure on me to take her to dances, something which did not attract me in the slightest. She gave me the ultimatum, come to dances with me or I will call it off! We discussed it a bit but we were both inflexible, partly because the business we were successfully building up often kept me till 8.30 or 9pm and to get cleaned up from a truly filthy job, was too much to entertain. As it was, I was turning up at their house after 9pm in my boiler suit - sometimes I had washed my hands and face and put on a clean boiler suit - it would have taken too long at that hour to get properly washed and changed. Not to mention the subsistence only wage I was being paid, but chaps similarly placed all complained about their father's not paying them enough! We parted as very good friends, she was one of a group of girls who might have influenced her? But that was that. I was bitterly disappointed.

In 1930 I bought the AC, 12hp car, that I had collected for Mr John Coward, an employee of the Midland Bank in 1926, direct from the factory at Thames Ditton. He was a number of years my senior and had started courting and distance compelled him to acquire a means of transport. Things came to a head in 1930, they had married and got a house, all at considerable expense, so the car had to go. I bought it and used it for two or three years as it was very handy to have a car and I made good use of it.

I also bought myself a new GTP Velocette and used it fairly successfully at a grass-track during that year, until it landed me in hospital in Whitehaven but I soon got over it. In 1931 Malcolm and I would build a bike ourselves. It was fitted with two 172cc Villiers Super Sports engines, a Moss four-speed gearbox, wall forks and the largest brakes commercially available. It ran well, was not very fast with a top speed of 60mph, but its traction was marvellous and, in the 1931 Sporty Boys Trial, was the only one to climb Walna Scar unassisted, due to its high traction at low engine speeds.

We decided that it was a bit under-powered and, talking to my friend, Kit Parker of Scott, AJS and Jowett fame, he asked me why I hadn't fitted a Scott engine, as they had built a few vertical twin-engines, of 498 and 650cc capacity and he knew they were not proceeding with the production. He then asked, "Would you like me to see if I can obtain one for you?" To which I replied, "Yes, I would."

Kit Parker was as good as his word. I went over to Saltaire in a car, saw the engine - a 650cc - and I noticed that it had three cylinder head gaskets on and they also gave me two spare connecting rods and a new crankshaft - hardened but not yet ground.

Malcolm and I built a new frame around this engine, this was in 1932. We made a new sub-frame unit which carried the engine, gearbox, (Moss four-speed with foot change), magdynamo and carburettor. This was installed in the motorcycle frame as one unit. The motorcycle frame was designed to support a specially made Serck radiator. It had Webb forks and was generally similar to the frame for the 344cc model of the previous year. I used the machine a number of times and everything seemed to be going well. The three cylinder head gaskets were removed, they were an eyesore and presumably they had been fitted by Scott for a valid reason, so we cut a replica gasket out of ³⁄₁₆" thick aluminium plate which held water and was no trouble. I never got round to asking why Scotts had fitted the three gaskets. Up to this time I don't think Malcolm had ridden the 650cc so he said, "I think I will take a day off and go down to Blackpool." I had no objection, he had ridden about town for about three years on the 344cc model (and others) without problems and I agreed whole-heartedly. This was going to be his first longish ride - he was going for the day, but for a variety of reasons mainly connected with the business, he was unable to leave until about 1.30pm, which was three or four hours later than he had intended. I saw him off, all seemed to be going well and he was followed by the usual Scott 'Yowl!' He was riding a fairly powerful machine and was probably pushing it on a bit. At the north end of Carnforth level, he passed the Oldham battery representative, who had called on us earlier that day. He recognised the machine and rider and he later expressed how well the machine was running, he also mentioned the blue haze from the exhaust - a feature of Scott engines at speed. A mile further along, he again came across them, this time both Malcolm and the machine were lying in the road, no other vehicle was involved, the machine had only suffered slight damage to the corner of the saddle and the rear number plate. Malcolm was taken to Royal Lancaster Infirmary where he died later that evening. A mechanic

Malcolm on the 1930 GTP Velocette on Helm, at Oxenholme. Price new, ready for the road £37. 10s. 0d

Malcolm outside the back of the Parish Church with the 1931 BAC as originally built and later adapted.

from the motorcycle shop in Carnforth, who had come out to the machine, gave it a kick start, one prod, the engine sprang into life and he immediately rode into the motorcycle shop and stated the machine was 'no worse'. I never rode it again. Our parents were distraught, Malcolm was only nineteen years old, the best of the three of us, much leaner and quite sensitive and always obliging. I can only blame lack of motorcycling experience and too powerful a machine. I gave up motorcycling until after the war when I was obliged to get a motorcycle to get to work, as I was refused a petrol ration for a car and I only got one for a bike after much arguing.

Laura had to take her annual holiday from the dental practice at the same time her father (a signalman) took his railway holiday and her mother took this opportunity to go for her annual fortnight at Rothesay, which she enjoyed and which was so beneficial for her - so Laura went with her every year to help her and to generally look after her. One of the things Mr Pinch always did was to send them a copy of 'The Westmorland Gazette', into which Malcolm's obituary notice was displayed (we had 'split up' in December 1928, so this was almost four years later), in the meantime I had never seen her.

Laura, being the kind and generous person she was, wrote a lovely letter of sympathy to me. She remembered Malcolm well and liked him a lot - she was obviously very moved and naturally I replied to Laura thanking her for her kind concern and of the shock it must have been to her to read the obituary notice. From that moment onwards, we became more attached to each other than previously and a year later we became engaged. I bought her the ring of her choice, a diamond cluster. She went home and showed it to her mother, who said, "It's lovely, he must have more money than sense!" We both began to save for our wedding, which we later decided to be on 10th October 1934. The significance being, that on this date we were both the same age, her birthday was on the 5th October 1909 and mine on the 19th October 1908 and for fourteen days we were both the same age and for that fortnight, she never forgot to remind me good naturedly, that I was no longer 'boss' for these fourteen days!

We were married at St Marks Church, Natland, about 11am on 10th October 1934 and the reception was held in the Oxenholme Mission Hall. (Many years ago the hall went out of use as a place of worship and was used for a long time as a garage for Billy Barnes, a small haulage contractor for his seven ton van). The catering for the reception was carried out by Jack Marshall and his French wife, everything being transported by vans from his shop, which was next door (north) of the

Wedding reception at Oxenholme Misson Hall on 10th October 1934.

Left to right: Kathleen Raffles, Kenneth Lees (best man), Joy Ingram, Bernard, Laura and Rachael Moorhouse. Note the sign - 'Faith brings Victory!'

Atkinson & Pollitt (Kendal photographers)

Westmorland Gazette Office. They provided for us very well. For the wedding my father took a new Armstrong Siddeley out of the showroom and had it licenced especially for the purpose. Jack Hutton was dressed appropriately and drove the car. My mother, of course, was the 'organiser' and did well, apart from forgetting to send a car to collect me from our house on Natland Road ('The Hutte'), and in the meantime Jack Hutton was making several laps of the lane, up to the bottom of Helm, via the railway bridge, turning left towards Kendal and then down the other lane to Natland. After this performance and in spite of some people saying, 'I was calling it off!' - someone remembered that no car had been sent for me and I could not have walked, just having had an operation on my left foot the day before. It all worked out in the end and Laura never doubted me. After Laura had changed out of her finery, we were taken down to 'The Hutte', where my car was stored ready for the 'off'. Then I found the keys to the garage had gone missing, it turned out Harold Simcoe (photographer with the Westmorland Gazette) had them and in the fracas to recover them, he fell heavily on the base of the Jones sewing machine. He was no match for me but I suppose he was about twice my age. No contest!

There was a hole in the garage door where a yale-type lock had previously been and when we went into the garage to go away we found the car to be literally swamped in confetti, nothing much we could do about it then. We had planned to be in the Viaduct Hotel, in Carlisle that night and we had to get rid of most of that mess. We went via the Lakes and turned left just before Thirlmere and round the back road and stopped on top of the dam at the north end of the lake. Here we both set to work to get rid of this mess of confetti. We finished this off and started again and got to Carlisle in reasonable time. When I arrived I wrote a letter to Harold Simcoe apologising for any injury he might have received, due to his practical joke going wrong.

The following day we went into Scotland and then across to the east coast at Jedburgh, where we stayed for bed and breakfast again. Next day we travelled south as far as Newcastle, where we stayed for that night. I don't remember precisely where we stayed every night but I remember as we approached London, probably about thirty miles away, the engine quite suddenly developed an ominous 'rattle'. I stopped the car in a convenient place at the roadside, opened the bonnet and realised immediately that it was the valve gear. I got my tools out (I never went anywhere without them), removed the valve rocker cover and found the noise to be emanating from the forward overhead camshaft bush. I took off the top half of the front camshaft bearing and found that the top half of the front camshaft bearing had 'run'. I realised immediately that the top half-bush is the one carrying the load in an ohc (overhead camshaft) engine - so I took out the top half of the bearing and in its place put the lower half of the bearing, this enabled us to drive into London and find an MG dealership, where I could buy another complete bearing. No further trouble was experienced on this account. We stayed in a Blackheath hotel in the south of London. Next day, we went to the south coast and we were motoring sedately between Rye and Hastings, when our windscreen was totally shattered on the driver's side. Laura was driving and she had a serviette spread on the top of her skirt, upon which was an assortment of unwrapped sweets (they did not all come wrapped then!), they were covered in shattered glass. I had to lift the serviette and its contents and tip them into the grass verge. Here again, safety glass was not a standard feature of cars in those days!

The cause of our predicament was simple. Pressure drills were breaking a trench up the middle of the road for a water main, one of the stones had become dislodged, flew up and broke our screen. I fixed up one of the side screens with cord to enable us to carry on as no-one we tried had a spare half-screen for an 'M' type MG. I don't remember whether we stopped for the night before we arrived in Penzance, we may well have done. However, in Penzance we stayed in a private house with a 'vacancies' sign in the window. We were made very welcome, so welcome in fact that the following day we went to Land's End (towards the end of October) but we did not stay very long as it was cold and the sea spray was blowing so we returned for another night in the house in Penzance. Again, I cannot remember all the places we stayed - but we did stay in Bideford. I sent a five gallon wooden cask of cider to my parents - in the event it was my brother, Bryan, who used to make frequent visits into the cellar, to draw off a mug of cider for himself! We then came up through Somerset and into South Wales. We did think of calling upon the Misses Maud and Winifred Horner, who had been headmistress and another mistress in the Kendal Girls' High School. I still have a photograph of their Clyno 13, which they called the 'pink-un', it was ordered as 'red' but it was a rather startlingly bright colour. The original engine in this car was replaced free of charge by Clyno, in their Wolverhampton factory. It was one of the only two cases I have ever encountered (the other was a Riley), where water from the water jacket seeped through into the inlet track. In the case of the Clyno, if the car was used every day it did not present a problem but if it stood in the garage from say Saturday or Sunday until Thursday (half day at school), it would not start because the plugs were wetted as soon as the engine was cranked.

Bernard's 1930 'M' Type MG - being stripped down for major overhaul, prior to putting into use - end of 1933. Laura used to take her mother out in it before they were married.

A few years later this car taking Summer Lodge whilst members of the Westmorland Motor Club. It never failed to climb this hill but with it's three speed gearbox, had nothing to spare.

Clyno 'Thirteen' of the Misses Maud and Winifred Horner, nicknamed the 'Pink-un'! Note the size of the front brakes. The Clyno had the best four wheel brakes of any popular make of car on the market at that time 1926.

From the Bristol area we came diagonally across Wales, via Builth Wells to Aberystwyth where the sea was very rough and noisy and the promenade was littered with stones, sand etc thrown up by the rough sea. We came further north, never very far from the sea, and finished up in Chester, where we had our last meal in a good restaurant - fresh fish and sauces etc, then back to Kendal before dark.

The first month of married life back in Kendal we stayed with my parents at 'The Hutte' but, even though the house was big, we knew these arrangements were not going to work. We scoured the 'to let' columns in the Gazette that week and saw a house, 9 Ford Terrace, offered for letting by Harry Walker. It had been occupied by his son-in-law, Jim Otway and his daughter, who was now required to live with them in their old age as they couldn't manage alone. We took it and, at the same time, I agreed to put electric lights into the house, with three pin plugs in all the rooms and on the landing. Whilst I am not an electrician, I did put the first electric system in Mr Pinch's house at Oxenholme and I had done a considerable amount at the garage as it grew and grew. We were fine on Ford Terrace and quite happy, though hard pressed financially. I still had our 'M' type MG which I stored in the garage where I worked sixty hours plus every week. About this time, perhaps two, possibly three years later, we saw the house exactly across the river from us, had a 'for sale' notice put up. It belonged to Ralph & Mrs Vause. He had been sent to work in their Lancaster office (printing trade) permanently, which put them in a position similar to ours - except we had no mortgage. We bought it through the Halifax Building Society where, due to parental pressure, I had opened an account a few years before we were married and which now stood us in good stead. We had enough for the deposit and the repayments if they did not exceed the 12/6d (62½p) per week we had been paying for rent. Unfortunately, there was no access from the rear, so no possibility to put up a garage, so our car was still garaged where I worked. Petrol in those days was only a little over 1/- (5p) per gallon.

Castle Mills on Aynam Road were no longer making woollen cloth and was now a carpet factory, owned by Goodacres. When Laura and I were married in 1934, father negotiated a deal with them on our behalf. He had been making patterns for the firm for some time and negotiated with them to provide us with carpets for our setting up house, in exchange for the patterns supplied - in other words he cancelled his invoice. I never knew the details but we were pleased to be provided with the carpets - which gave us many years of service, in fact it was only when we moved to Oxenholme after the death of Laura's father, that we bought replacements for the larger house.

Laura used to go to see Miss Gedye at the Halifax Building Society with our remittance regularly and we were never in arrears. One day Laura went into the Yorkshire Bank to draw out the payment to take to the Halifax. Mr Young, the then manager of the Yorkshire Bank, came up to Laura and asked if she was being attended to? She replied, "Yes, I have just spoken to the young man who was here. I have just come to draw the money for the Halifax Building Society." "Oh!" he said, "You won't need to bother about that now!" She did not understand. He went on to explain, "Your father has been in and paid off the whole amount." This was in the region of four thousand pounds and an exceedingly generous gesture. This immediately put us on a better footing financially as 12/6d per week made a vast difference to us but all the same we remained very cautious.

I remember, soon after this, a tool salesman came with a van full of the most desirable tools any mechanic could wish for. Some of the men in the garage made purchases and I was very tempted to buy a Gedore ½" square drive socket wrench set, in a steel box, covering all popular English, American and French sizes. I went home on my bicycle to see what Laura thought, she was undoubtedly the Chancellor of the Exchequer, so I must get her permission first because she was so very careful with our spending. She agreed that I should have it, which I still have to this day.

Christine, our daughter, was born on the 10th July 1938 and some two years later our son, Peter was born. They were both healthy children and Laura did a good job bringing them up because, as usual, I was at work most of the time.

Laura's father, Jack Pinch, was a grand fellow. We were living in our own little house at 12 Natland Road. With war rapidly approaching, and us with one infant and another on the way, I decided to make a cellar under the house. First I cut out a section of floor boards in the hall at the foot of the stairs and supported the floor by extra timbers around the hole and made the board I removed, into a hinged trap door. I suppose the amount of air space under the floor was about nine inches. Under the trap door Mr Pinch and I together dug out the earth to a depth of six feet over a small area. Having done this, we dug out straight towards the north wall to a width of two feet - we went right under the concrete foundation to the outside, this we then shuttered up to within about nine inches of the foundation. It was then filled with concrete and allowed to set for ten days before it was filled right to the foundation with the mixed concrete rammed in, then retained with more shuttering.

Who lives there - picture of Kirkland in 1936 with Miss England in foreground. Properties listed - (A) Roper's house; (B) Clement's house; (C) Keates house; (D) Keates shop; (E) Everson's house, with double fronted shop underneath; (F) Chamber's house; (G) Well's house; (H) Ferguson's 1st and 2nd floor accommodation, with Blair's smithy on ground floor. The main large garage doors are to the left of the picture and are not shown.

The ill fated 'Miss England' speedboat on the way to Windermere to attempt the world water speed record in 1936. The driver had stopped at lunch time to enquire the way. When parked, unfortunately, a passing vehicle 'rolled' the driver along the side of it, quite unaware of the man's presence - he had passed so closely to the vehicle. The driver escaped serious injury and was able to continue his journey. Note the solid lorry tyres, at that time were in regular use. Sadly the record breaker Major H. O. D. Seagrave met his death in this attempt, when his boat hit a submerged piece of driftwood, the boat was travelling at full speed at the time.

We then turned completely round and did the same underneath the wall between the dining room and the pantry, which also supported the staircase. We never did more than two feet in width at any one time and we always went to opposite sides of the peculiar shaped cellar we were erecting, so there was never any risk of the detached house collapsing on top of us. All the earth removed was wheeled out, up the passage, through the front door and deposited on the garden, where we had to get a man with a lorry to remove it. We mixed all our own concrete. Sand and cement were delivered by a builders' merchant. The result was a peculiar-shaped room and we had to make an escape route should the house be collapsed by enemy action. We made a passage underneath the house and came up under the path outside, here we placed a large square manhole frame and cover, which could be pushed up from inside and had two lifting handles on the outside. It was never locked and neighbours were informed of the existence of the cellar, as were some of the garage staff. Happily it had never to be put into service. We had a large drain hole in the floor (the lowest point) just in case we got water in from any source, burst pipe or the river not far away. The River Kent (hence Kent Dale - Kendal) was one of the fastest flowing rivers in England. When in spate, the arches of Nether Bridge are completely filled and I have seen two inches of water on top of the former Romney Road Bridge, when it was a foot bridge. On such an occasion I lifted the trap door to the cellar and found the water to be only one foot below the floor boards, it was a good job I left the drain away hole or it would have taken quite a long time to disperse. As it was it was almost totally gone 24 hours later.

The 650cc bike on which Malcolm had the accident remained leaning against the wall of the garage until the outbreak of war. Many men were called up and bus services became less reliable and one of Woolleys (Windermere) employees who lived in Sedbergh was having problems getting to work. He persuaded me to sell it to him, which I did. Not very long after, he was 'called up' had nowhere to leave the bike, so bought it back and, by coincidence, British Rail closed the Kendal Goods Yard and transferred their vehicles to Grange. John Airey, a pal of mine, had to go to Grange to work. He was a Scammell driver and he bought the bike to travel to work at Grange from whence deliveries to Kendal were made. I had no part in handling the price then agreed upon but John used the bike daily whatever the weather. We could hear John going to work from further along Natland Road, up to Nether Bridge, then down the other side of the river as far as Prizet - the distinctive 'Scott yowl!'

Family photo of Bernard and Laura, with Peter and Christine - Summer Lodge, Natland Road, 1944

1939-45 WAR YEARS

Everyone knows that Germany invaded Poland and were utterly ruthless. Britain was committed to defend Poland by some treaty or another and that was how Britain became involved. According to authority, Britain expected to be a target for German bombers from the outset but there was a phoney war period, where only Poland suffered. Apparently Poland was to be totally over-run and subjugated before Hitler's next move. My father offered to set up making munitions and letters to the Ministry of Supply fell on deaf ears for a considerable time. Call-ups were being issued in the 19-25 age groups and there was the black-out. Many of our staff were called up and went into Lancashire munitions factories - presumably government-sponsored factories. Elsie Clark, our secretary, was called up and whenever we saw her she was kitted out in khaki. The last of our men to go was Jardine Scaife. Bryan, my brother, was also called up (1st Malitia) and returned without serious injury at the end of the war.

In the meantime, we carried on with reduced staff and very little business. The motorists of the time knew headlamp masks were compulsory and, to fill in the time until we were awarded a munitions contract at the beginning of 1940, I and one apprentice occupied our time by making headlamp masks of our own design, which complied with the laws regarding the amount of light emitted and its direction. Father, as I said, had already advised the Ministry of Supply of our 1914-18 war production and quoted the names of the two principle recipients of our manufactures which went by rail to William Beardmore & Co, of Paisley and Dobbie Forbes Ltd, of Larbert, in Stirlingshire. Nothing was heard for an age (so it seemed), eventually in 1939 we were sent drawings of shell bases to be made out of fifty-five ton high tensile steel. These were to be used for twenty-five pounder gas shells and were to be given Priority 1A, which meant that any equipment in the form of cutting tools were to be made available to us - excepting the actual machines. We already had three SS/SC lathes (sliding, surfacing and screw-cutting), one by Burton Griffiths, one by Greenwood and the one we called the Windermere lathe because that is where it came from. All the material we used in production was a free issue - our only charge to the Authorities was for the manufacturing processes.

Z Crabtree in 1939. Note the pile of tyres for sale

Inside the garage 1939 - Riley belonging to Derek Dakeyne Cannon, an Armstrong Siddeley and our taxi covered up.

My father, who was medically unfit for service in WW1 and was too old for WW2, was the brains behind our set up. We spent the first three months in making special heavy duty tool holders, for seven lathes and also heavy cast iron stop frames, for limiting the travel of both the main slides and the cross slides in both directions, making our own collet chucks. We made new spindles and nuts for the thread millers, for different thread pitches and even for left-hand, right-hand threads.

We also made various drilling jigs for priming holes and for keyholes to match wrenches we had never seen - items too technical and varied to describe. Throughout the whole period of our involvement we received monthly visits from a Mr Allonby, an engineer from the War Department, who advised us on types of cutting steels available and helped us to solve problems of balancing the output of our machines and was able to help in this way by finding lathes, etc, lying unused in other garages. I remember on our first contract the first operation involved the removal of very heavy cuts of fifty-five ton high tensile steel and we had already two lathes on this operation, but were still finding later operations were being held up. We had already bought one extra lathe for this operation from Keswick and we pointed out this hold up to Mr Allonby. He went out to look for another lathe and came back in about an hour and said, "Will you go to Crofts Garage, they have a heavy lathe there which the mechanic says they never use, and it may help you get your production volume up. I have made arrangements for you to collect it but I have been unable to fix a price, as the owner of the premises has been called up. The arrangement I have made is this, you are to collect the machine and get it to work. After the war you will have to agree with Mr Croft, on either a rental charge for the time you have it or a purchase price." In the event Mr Croft came back from the war and he was acquainted with the situation and in reply, said he was 'glad to see the back of it as it was just so much garage furniture' - we then agreed a price.

As I pointed out earlier, father spent most of WW2 in the garage and the office looking after the business side. As far as I am aware, we were the only public service garage in Kendal a hundred per cent engaged in war production.

I got my call-up papers and I had to appear at the Organ Works in Kendal, which was being used at that time as a recruiting station, to pass the doctor and the Board so, for once, I did not go to work in my dirty overalls, I went in a suit. I went to work as usual and at the appointed time, having seen that all the machines were working well, I was descending the stairs from the first floor works and met Mr Allonby coming up. It was the first time he had ever seen me with a suit on, so he asked where I was going. I replied, "The Organ Works!" He obviously did not know the inference, so I told him I had got my call-up papers. "Have you volunteered?" he asked. I replied, "No!" He then said, "You will have to go now. When you leave they will give you a paper." Taking out a long self-addressed envelope he said, "Put the paper in this envelope and get it in the post today." I did just that and never heard any more. If I had gone to war the job would have stopped!

The roof over the machine shop was one third glass, in sheets seven feet by two feet, on galvanised glazing bars. These were blacked out at the appropriate times by seven feet by $\frac{3}{16}$" ply wood sheets, which slid on 3" x 2"wooden spars, fixed to the four purlins. It only took five or six minutes to put the black-out in position, all the other lower windows were painted black on the inside. Here again father's genius was at work!

We also brought in the two thread millers we had during WW1, which were outside after many moves and had eventually ended up on the scrap heap. Unlike the other six machines that were made, as previously described, father had at least insisted that whenever a scrap man was removing metal from our premises, they were always strictly informed that these two machines were not to be taken. The fact that they eventually ended up outside was, to say the least, unfortunate and the moves were caused by the constant enlargement of the garage premises. The main iron casting of very robust proportions had not suffered too badly but all the steel items had and we had to make replacements for all of them and, by the time we were given war production contracts, they were again serviceable and accurate. Many more hundreds of thousands of components were made with internal and external threads of the highest quality, as evidenced by the fact that we remained in production until VJ Day. During the whole of this period, never did we have even one complaint, or even one reject. Internal inspection was carried out by our own female operators, trained in our own works and whose ages ranged between fourteen and sixty-four years. We had twenty women who worked for us - Ivy Orme, (about 60 years old and she was the last to leave at the end of the war), Elsie Simm, Evelyn Hine (17), Letty Pinfold (all the time), Lila Law, Hilda Bigland, Bertha Sharp and Irene Clement are the only ones I can remember.

All the female staff we employed were trained in our own works and on our own machines. They worked on the first floor at the back (later the showroom). There were serious restrictions on labour of any kind during this period and all employees had been directed to us by the local

Bryan Crabtree

Labour Exchange and, what is more, if their labour ceased to be required, they had to be sent to the Labour Exchange to be redirected to where they could be fully employed. This happened on several occasions when we were awaiting deliveries of steel bars, steel stampings, iron castings and brass castings. Some of these were delivered to us in full railway wagon loads of twelve tons, some others in smaller quantities.

Letty's daughter was just fourteen years of age and came straight to us after leaving school and asked to be taken on. She was given instruction immediately - we did this because her mother was already one of our star hands on a medium heavy lathe. She pressed for instruction, her mother agreed and, as it happened, we had at that moment a light lathe - still 6" centres and SS & SC. The girl was delighted and became a useful member of our staff. I remember though, when she was learning she touched a belt and got her fingers nipped! Taking our female operators as a whole, they did a magnificent job in a completely strange environment and it is my belief that if we had, by some magical means, been able to change them instantly into male operatives, such as those on our pre-war staff - production would have gone down rather than up! They did a magnificent job; they did not really understand what they were doing, but simply obeyed their instructions to the letter. I know this to be true because, at some time or other, I had to take over the lathe, drilling machine or thread miller without notice, whenever boyfriend or husband came on leave and, concentrating as I did, I could only beat the one hour's performance by one unit!

They started work at 8am and finished at 5.30pm, with an hour off for lunch (between 12.30 -1.30) and Saturday 8am until midday. I used to go to the works a full half hour before the 'girls'. This was particularly essential in the cold weather, partly because all but one of our eight lathes were old but, in the right hands and with the right set-up and management, were still quite capable of accurate works and this was proved over and over again. The early start was so that the electric motors could be started fifteen minutes before 8am and all the lathes, except the one new one from America, be set in motion to break the oil film adequately before the girls arrived. Otherwise the oil film was so viscous that the lathes ran at a speed far below that required for efficient working. This in turn was the cause of the components being torn out of the lathe chucks with disastrous results to the cutters (lathe tools). For three of the lathes it involved complete regrinding to the correct contour of four cutters and as these cutters were Wimet (cemented carbide) if anything went wrong, it was an expensive business and very time consuming, as it took at least half an hour to set the machine up again, to produce work consistently so, if more than one machine was stopped, the off work time was multiplied accordingly, as I was the only person available to set the machine up again.

Basically therefore, before any work could commence, the machine had to be correctly set up. This involved the making of patterns in wood for a cast iron frame of square section, with suitably heavy lugs downward facing at the front, drilled and tapped ½" Whitworth thread, to make contact with the headstock. This was to limit the forward movement of the saddle at a precise point, and similar lugs and stops to limit the lateral movement of the cross slide. In this manner a girl, who had never even seen a lathe in her life, could be producing accurate work after little over half an hour's instruction. All this preparation took time but it paid off handsomely over the entire war period. It was capable of being adjusted to suit various other types of components. Father studied the drawings of every new type of article we were to manufacture and came up with satisfactory designs to comply with every requirement. Each new component we were called upon to make had its own problems to be solved - and they were solved.

The smallest items we were called upon to manufacture were the delay caps for Howitzer shells. This material came to us in the form of 1" diameter bright steel bar, about sixteen feet in length. The components had a finished length of 0.60" plus or minus .005". I remember our female operators, including inspection and packing, produced 3,360 perfect finished delay caps in one 47 hour week and every week thereafter.

In fact one of the contracts, involving round bar steel of varying lengths, was supplied to us for processing and, at the end of a 50,000 run, we had sufficient bar material left to produce a further 160 components which we processed and delivered. We knew that our next contract was for an entirely different component, and if they had found any rejects amongst the 50,000 already delivered and had then demanded replacements from us, we would have found it impossible to provide them, all our machines having been converted to the new production.

Some weeks later Mr Parker (in charge of Preston Ironworks, to whom all our production had been delivered on a weekly basis), telephoned and spoke to me, telling me that we had exceeded the contract by one hundred and sixty and that he had been trying to obtain payment for us for the 'additional to contract' components but that he had failed to manage it.

I told him that was all right as we had only worked up all the material we had been supplied with, just in case they found any rejects in the components already supplied. He replied, "Mr Crabtree, we have never ever found one unit amongst the many thousands supplied that did not pass our scrutiny." After all, not only had we inspection on a machine basis but we had our own resident inspector, who had strict instructions never to pass any unit which did not comply with all the limit gauges. His salary was paid for by HM Government, but that inspector was a waste of labour - because nothing ever was rejected. On top of this we had a one day per week visit from an official CIA Inspector (Chief Inspector of Armaments), whose duty it was to recheck any item our own final inspection had held back for rechecking.

As I said, we made many hundreds of thousands of warlike stores in the 1939-45 war and without a single reject. This does not mean we never spoilt any work piece, but nothing ever got past inspection. We had some problems but these were largely caused by 220 tons of burnt forgings - I need not tell you where they came from but the fact remains that at one time we had upwards of 10,000 chemical shell bases that were rejected by our own inspection due to defects in the forgings. We notified the receiving station of our problems who said, "Continue production and we will send an inspector to examine them as soon as possible." That 'soon as possible' turned out to be many weeks, that was the reason we accumulated the 10,000 odd. Incidentally the inspector who came accepted the whole lot - the fault was not ours but in the forgings.

My working day was from 7.30am until 9pm, or even later if someone was absent for any reason (13½-14 hrs), and generally Saturday and Sunday afternoon working almost entirely on munitions. Looking back, I do not understand quite how it was that I was never slightly involved in the costings, expenses or receipts. Father paid the wages so presumably that, plus the cost of electricity and tools, gave him all the information he needed. I was however given a freehand in acquiring any additional machines or tools we required and, when we were agreed, they were acquired as quickly as was then possible.

We weren't wealthy, my wage had never been high in spite of the hours I put in every week, never less than sixty and frequently considerably more even throughout the war. They were long days, seven days a week, to keep production up and my wage was a flat £5 per week throughout. I saw Percy Harris, a pal of mine in town one day during the war and we were exchanging information about our respective war work jobs. Percy told me he was getting £15 per week flat and he was surprised and shocked when I told him I got £5 per week. I told my father of our conversation and what Percy was getting at Standards. His response was, "Then perhaps you had better go and work at Standards!" He knew I couldn't, I was tied to working at Crabtrees! I didn't realise the full situation until afterwards but, during all this wartime work, we didn't get paid very quickly and father had to make arrangements for a big overdraft and I should imagine all contractors had suffered the same fate. During this time mother was doing a lot of the office work - so we were all very busy.

In case you wonder what Standards had to do with it - after the air raid on Coventry, Standards moved to Kendal and equipped Castle Mills with engineering machinery and they produced finished cylinder heads from castings supplied for the Bristol Pegasus radial poppet-valve aero engines. Bristol also made Bristol Hercules sleeve-valve radial aero engines but Standards had nothing to do with these.

A variety of other batches of work, generally one or two hundred were made from brass round or hexagon bar, supplied by Gilkes, together with detailed drawings. One order we did for Gilkes, was for high tensile steel tapered bolts for a 'gold mine in Peru'. Many of these items involved taking one or perhaps two machines off our regular production schedule, which unfortunately involved overtime or even weekend working under pressure. But we were all in the job together to achieve optimum results. Probably Gilkes helped us when we required iron castings at short notice for the manufacture of jigs etc. On the whole and looking back, we worked together very much as an unofficial team.

As I mentioned earlier, my father had regularly done pattern making for Isaac Braithwaite (IBIS Works) and Gilkes and during the war years we still helped one another. Gilkes of course had their own iron foundry and, as mentioned, supplied any iron castings we needed. IBIS supplied us with any unusual sizes and sections of steel from their extensive stocks and we were never disappointed. On the other hand, although they were both working direct for the Ministry of Supply, they came across certain items, such as special nuts in brass or cast iron which had internal and sometimes external threads, requiring to be lathe cut by means of a special single point tool, which we did.

'Jock' Hutton, (not to be confused with Jack Hutton from Crabtrees) Gilkes works' manager, frequently came into our works on Saturday afternoons to weigh up form, ask questions and pass comments. I was at their works a few times but then I did not have Saturday afternoons free as he did. In spite of our age difference, he must have been almost twice my age, I respected his judgement but I suppose with my relative youth,

At work in the machine room at the garage. Derek Elvey is on the left, Bernard in the foreground boring a four cylinder block with the Hall Toledo boring bar and George Scattergood on the right

my mind was the more agile and perhaps was able to respond to changed circumstances more rapidly.

One Saturday morning, Jock came round when I was setting up all the various machines for the following week's hitch-free production. We were at that time sawing off about 5,000 blanks per week from steel bar and some of the five power saws were working - building up a buffer stock of blanks for the following week. He came over to where I was working and asked if we could saw (for Gilkes) blanks from this stainless steel bar. They had tried in their own works and made little progress, so they contacted Short Brothers (of Flying Boat fame) who had a works between Windermere and Ambleside. This works was built in a wood for concealment and on the edge of the lake for launching. The works were equipped with the very latest machinery and they told Short's manager of the problem and asked if they could help. They agreed to 'have a go' and a length of the bar was sent in Gilkes' van.

Jock was very fair with me and told me that Shorts spent a lot of time and effort and had done very serious damage to their Wicksteed hydraulic saw and some of the special cutters. They were waiting for the cost of the rectification of the machine to come through but they were warned it would be expensive. Jock said if we could 'have a go', they would pay 10/- (50p) each for cutting off the blanks. This sounded good to me, so he sent a three foot length of the bar to test.

I had already told him I could not lock-up any one of our five machines for more than a few hours on a Saturday, when all our female staff were shopping and doing essential housework, washing etc.

I also agreed to 'have a go' and the following Saturday afternoon when I was alone in our works, I took the jig off our Rapidor saw and fitted a new blade and set the load on the saw to maximum - at the end of 2½ hours continuous sawing it had barely penetrated ½". So I had to put my thinking cap on and went far beyond Rapidor's instruction regarding the pressure on the blade and fitted another one, this time a resharpened four threads per inch blade and we made progress and were able to get Gilkes over their difficulty, at some cost to ourselves but we gained experience.

As a matter of interest, we were buying our 16", 14" and 12" power blades from Rex Hacksaw, Tool and Manufacturing Company, London, and we had already proved that it paid us to use a blade for one day only, remove it and return them to Rex Hacksaw who then resharpened them. They then performed better than ever and that became our regular practice, only we did not of course return them singly!

We were now getting towards the end of the war when we were suddenly approached by McNeill's of Barrow (probably advised of our capability to produce) to share a contract with them to produce HE shell (high explosive) bases in large numbers. The blanks were delivered in sacks to McNeill's and we had to arrange to collect our supply of blanks from them. This we did through the co-operation of one of our pre-war customers, Messrs Chas Cumpstey & Son who were tallow manufacturers in Kendal and whose lorry we knew toured all butchers shops in Cumberland, collecting bones from which the tallow was made They collected blanks as well as delivering the finished components weekly. These were for high explosive shell bases, steel stampings ⁵⁄₃₂" thick, bevelled on one edge. On one occasion the suppliers of the blanks got behind and McNeill's hogged the supply. The driver for Cumpsteys, Jack Lancaster, came and said he had nothing for us - so I telephoned about this and they agreed to release a supply, so it fell to me to go to Barrow with our breakdown vehicle to collect them. We were then able to resume production, which by that time was held up. No further such interruption occurred during the remainder of the contract.

That we had been held up for supplies of materials we were to process had occurred for several reasons, amongst which were enemy action delaying rail transport, late delivery from Drop Forgings Manufacturers and other supplies of raw materials from manufacturers for a whole variety of reasons. As an illustration of the results of these delays, we had on one occasion a longish hold up and had to put operatives 'on to the Labour Exchange!' This as I said was a wartime instruction that 'unoccupied labour must sign on'. On that occasion one of our 'girls', Bertha Sharp, probably in her thirties, was reallocated to another works in Kendal by the Labour Exchange. The new employer asked where she had worked and what work she had been doing? She replied that she had been a full time drilling machinist at Crabtree's and the work was 'jigged.'

The new employer 'Gilkes', knew of our war effort and the type and quality of the work being carried out. As a result, she was immediately placed on drilling work and within the first ten days she was 'scalped'. Bertha was in hospital for a very long time and had an area of scalp about the size of an old 5/- piece that would not heal. I know this from her friend who was recalled, after we received a lorry load of forgings and resumed work on her machine. Incidentally, in spite of her friend being 'scalped', Hilda Bigland, also had her hair pulled off in our works in a similar incident, when her hair became wrapped on a vertical spindle. Fortunately, Hilda had a narrow escape. When we asked the doctor why this girl was not 'scalped' as her friend had been, his interesting reply was, that her hair was 'not in good condition', which caused it to break, rather than pull off the skin with the hair. She was lucky and was back on the same machine by the beginning of the following week. There was, and had been, a large notice up in the works, 'All girls must wear Dutch bonnets'. They were made from blue cotton linen which we supplied. This instruction was disobeyed from time to time and even when it was obeyed, it was being disobeyed in principle, by leaving the front hair uncovered - vanity I suppose, but there were no spectators who cared a jot!

On another occasion, our star operator on the two thread millers somehow managed to have a thread cut right across her middle finger nail. I cannot imagine how she managed that! I think they were the only two accidents of any note that we suffered, apart from a packer hitting a finger, instead of the nail in the lid of an ammunition box.

During the war, we also stored overnight and did some work for British Insulated & Callenders Cables (BICC), who had two six-wheel lorries and a four-wheel lorry stored with us and West's Piling & Construction had a five ton Bedford. They used these vehicles when they were engaged in erecting electricity pylons and overhead high tension cables, from the electricity sub-station at Natland to Barrow-in-Furness, for ship building and heavy engineering. They were trying to rush this work through, but had problems with a lot of soft ground. This was also very important war work, although not part of our contract, and any time I spent on this work had to be made up by even more over-time and usually meant me working at night or father covering for me. BICC vehicles were rigid six-wheel, four-wheel drive vehicles. I remember one of the rear axles of one of the vehicles failed. These vehicles were absolutely invaluable for crossing the boggy land to be traversed and without them the job would not have been possible.

On another occasion one of West's Piling & Construction Bedford vehicles broke down one night. It was left overnight in the middle of boggy land and was towed out by one of BICC's vehicles, only to be found that it was frozen up and that its cylinder block was frost cracked and would not hold water. BICC towed this vehicle into our garage with the request that it should be repaired with all speed, as the piling job was being delayed by its absence. So I removed the engine and dismantled it and sent the cylinder block to Craghill & Co, one of our trade friends in Kendal, with the request that they repair the block as quickly as possible. They did just that but in the process they pre-heated the block to such a temperature that the white metal camshaft bushes 'ran'. It was only when the repaired block was returned to us and assembly commenced, that I realised the absence of camshaft bearings and could only assume what had happened. New white metal bushes were not available and the only alternative for us was to draw a phosphor bronze bar from our stores and to manufacture a new set of bushes, unfortunately (as is often the case with camshaft bushes) they were all of different sizes, the reason for this was to facilitate the fitting of the camshaft. It had been a big job but it was successfully completed. Whilst I was thus engaged, father was able to keep the munition production running smoothly.

On another occasion, I was called out by West's Piling to a pylon site in the middle of a field to deal with a stationary engine they could not start. It proved to be magneto trouble which I was able to repair. Whilst I was there, they demonstrated to me the depth to which these large reinforced concrete piles are driven, by lighting a screwed up newspaper and dropping it down the hole, it seemed to take an age to reach the bottom. That particular pile was one hundred and eight feet deep, one of the deepest in the world at that time. I won't go on to describe how these piles are inserted and then provided with a core of reinforced concrete, but it's a truly wonderful process. The thing was they had to dig down until they got something solid - so it all depended on the type of land on which they were working.

The only other 'private work' I did from the end of 1939 to VJ day, was keeping a couple of doctors' cars and one commercial travellers car (an AJS 9) running, all of which involved more overtime - over an ordinary eighty hour week. The AJS 9 belonged to an old customer, who had been 'chasing' me for weeks to attend to his car, bang in the middle of the war. So I arranged for him to bring his car in a week on Saturday and leave it until Monday, this was about midsummer. My wife and two children hardly ever saw me. I was away before 7.30 in the morning on my bicycle and was very seldom home before nine o'clock at night. The kids were still in bed when I went out and were back in bed before I returned. So I thought it would be a good opportunity to give them a treat!

The weather was fine and hot so my wife and children decided to have a dip in Killington Tarn, and myself and Evelyn Hine, one of the girls from our works, who had had some instruction on cars all went along. It was of course illegal use of petrol. I packed the car with washing-off brushes, steel tray, paraffin, grinding paste, cleaning rags and we set off from our works and made our way to the west side of Killington Tarn, on a little used narrow access lane. I found a level spot to mend the AJS 9 when we got there and for the kids to play safely.

Evelyn and I then got to work. We had the cylinder head and manifolds off quite soon, we had brought lots of tools with us. We removed all the valves and springs and had taken the precaution of spreading copies of the Westmorland Gazette under the car, just in case we dropped something and to absorb any oil drips. All went well and we had the decarbonizing and valve grinding completed by late afternoon. Evelyn then washed her dirty hands in the tarn, tucked her clothes inside her knickers and went into the water. I didn't need much encouragement and I too went into the water for a well-earned dip. It made a welcome change from the austere life we were forced to endure due to war conditions.

The two doctors and the commercial traveller referred to have been dead for some years and Evelyn last we heard of her was living in Blackpool. She used to call on us often when she was visiting her parents (now deceased) and her sisters, Mary and Gladys, who still live in Kendal. An interlude to be remembered in a war torn Europe over such a long period. We were not spotted on our 'illegal' war journey, total mileage about ten!

I remember an occasion in the 1930s, when Mr Hutchinson of Crook ordered a two-seater Armstrong Siddeley 15 and he wanted to go to the factory with me to collect it. We went together by train. I probably had the most alarming ride of my life coming home. He was not particular which side of the road he was using and to go into a blind corner in the middle of the road was the norm - we did not, by the grace of God, have an accident, how we missed, I'll never know! As a matter of interest and something to talk about, I asked him why he wanted a two-seater. His reply rather surprised me. He said, "Well, you know where I live, whilst my house is detached, there are a pair of semis next door and as soon as I get my car out to go into Kendal, one or other of them appears on their doorsteps with their hat and coat on, wanting a lift into Kendal!" Human nature?

His next car was an Armstrong Siddeley 17 Sportsman Coupé, with self-changing, four-speed gearbox, and Newton centrifugal clutch. He had bought this car in 1938 and it was in new condition with very low mileage. He was very car proud and very careful with it - and never had an accident on the road in spite of his erratic driving!

The war came along and private motoring was banned. Mr Hutchinson always kept a can of petrol in his garage 'just in case'. When the war was imminent he made his petrol stock up to two cans (four gallons) in order that he would from time to time be able to run the engine, to prevent deterioration, (something which was a very real

War service with the Auxilliary Fire Service (AFS), pictured inside the Fire Station, Aynam Road, Kendal. Bernard is on the extreme right on 2nd row. W Fulton Pennington dressed in coat (5th left 2nd row). Sergeant L Heap, 7th from left 2nd row

menace for those who simply locked their cars away). He realised that if he was to avoid a flat battery he would have to start the engine by hand and, as cars in 1938 were supplied with starting handles for emergency use, he brought his handle along to us and asked to have a rotating hand-grip made to make it more comfortable to use. This we did and all went well for the first year but, later on, one dreadful occasion, he had forgotten to ensure that the gear was in neutral. With a self-changing gearbox, it is essential to select neutral and then to depress the clutch pedal. It appears that he had failed to complete this manoeuvre, he had set all the controls and went to the front of the car with the starting handle, gave it a swing and the engine started as usual. Had he jumped to one side at this moment he would not have been trapped but he lingered, as a man in his sixties is permitted to do. The engine speeded up and trapped him by both legs against the end wall of the garage and as the engine speed increased, so did the engagement of the Newton clutch increase the pressure on his legs. The garage was remote from the house by some thirty yards and Mrs Hutchinson did not hear his calls for help, and it was only when she went out to bring him in for his lunch that she found him there trapped and with both legs broken. She switched off the engine and got help. I don't remember him ever driving again.

W Fulton Pennington, was looking for men with an engineering background to serve in the fire service during the war. I was enlisted with Bill Rogerson, from Craghills Garage, amongst others and was appointed leading fireman. There were about six of us in a unit and there were a number of units, based at the then Aynam Road Fire Station. We used to practice with fire hoses and pumps on Gooseholme. We did a week's night duty on a rota basis every four to six weeks. This was fitted in with my garage work and continued for the duration of the war. I can't remember our unit ever being called out. One of the units, I remember was called to Manchester to help with the air raid damage. They were there for three days and were never fed. They were pleased to get home, needless to say!

Some of Crabtree's garage staff about 1950.
Left to right: Ron Elvey, Mr Simmonds, Phil Chapman, Leslie Wilson, German mechanic and Derek Elvey

AFTER THE WAR TO THE 1960s

After the war the only staff immediately available to us, were two of the lady munitions workers, who had been kept on continuously right from their original engagement to the very end of the war production phase (Ivy Orme and Evelyn Hine). They had as a result of instruction become the most proficient of the whole munitions team and had, during the brief periods when we ran out of raw materials (forgings, castings, bar steel, brass and stainless steel), been working on general vehicle repairs and, when we were re-tooling after completion of the several various large contracts, were kept on our work-force to give such assistance as they were able to. When there was nothing for them that they were able to handle, we put the two of them into the garage and with the minimum of time possible spent instructing them, they were given relatively straightforward jobs, like decarbonizing four cylinder, water-cooled, car engines. They were not rapid but they learned and a good deal of checking of their work was required before release. The Aero Minx that I had bought and stripped down to bare chassis and which was standing on trestles, was one of the jobs I gave them to clean down and paint the chassis with black paint. They did not like doing this dirty work and not such a congenial atmosphere as in the machine shop, where there were up to twenty workers and in a warm environment with coke-fired stoves. The garage, in contrast, was a large wide open space without any form of heating and they came under the gaze of motorists and drivers of vehicles on their way to the toilets. So they did not stay long and the Aero Minx was not much nearer completion. A former member the Westmorland Motor Club came in one day and, seeing the car in its dismantled state, became interested. The chassis by this time was completely ready to receive the body but I had no time to work on it, as my father was not very well and I could see little prospect of my getting around to completing the job. So when Geoffrey Tedcastle offered me a price which I thought to be fair, I let him have it and he got someone with a flat lorry to take it away. I never saw the car again and I certainly never saw the purchaser driving the car. I never knew where it went or what its future was.

A friend and previous employee came in on his demob from the Air Force and told me he had bought a small garage near Coleshill and wanted to buy a lathe. So I sold him the 6" SS & SC Burton Griffiths lathe, for £35. On another occasion a contractor working on the Milk Marketing Board site came in and wanted to hire a power hacksaw. I managed to sell him one of the motorised Kingley machines for £60. Yet a third sale was made to Hayes & Parkinson, of one of the two Pollard drilling machines, bench type with No. 1 Morse taper and a 3000 rpm motor which, for woodworking, was an ideal speed. We had used them for drilling ³⁄₃₂" diameter holes in steel. That was the end of our sales of equipment, all at knock down prices.

Because of ammunition manufacture, we had been out of the motor trade right from the beginning of 1940 until about November 1945, in fact we were still in war production for a while after VJ Day. Then it became necessary to put our efforts into trying to win back our share of the motor business, which had had to be discarded due to war production, and our pre-war staff who, with the exception of Mr Hewitson who resided on the premises (in the flat above the garage), had been taken for war service, even two girls from the office. Mr Hewitson was kept on right through the war; he was petrol and oil attendant and garage man. This in fact meant that he supplied all the essential customers with petrol, diesel and lubrication oils; he also arranged the admission of essential vehicles into our premises for storage overnight - we had certainly the largest floor area available of any such premises in the town. For example, there were food distribution vans by Huntley & Palmer and Danish Bacon Co and SPD, plus casuals on their way to their various destinations. We even stored the occasional Queen Mary (long loaders) which were very competently driven by WAAF girls that were carrying damaged and sometimes new aircraft wings and the occasional fuselage to the places where they were required. So, at least our garage premises were performing an important service provided by the one man employed.

After the war, my family and I moved to Moorfields, Oxenholme (which had been Laura's parents' home) and of course that immediately meant I'd a longer journey to work. I used a bicycle for a short time whilst I made application for a petrol ration, which was turned down. I applied again and was again turned down. The fact that I had very uncertain hours carried no weight - not that I was called out frequently during the night to breakdowns. I was bemoaning my position amongst some friends and someone suggested that I could get a ration for a motorcycle - very bravely (or stupidly, depending how you look at it), I bought a new 350 transverse, twin Douglas from Frank Walker and applied for a petrol ration - it was turned down. So I again applied and put forward more arguments why it was essential, supported by customers' signatures. I got a modest ration - so it was legal to use the Douglas.

It was a good-looker in its day, but completely gutless. I remember, when it was new, running up to Windermere Golf Club at what I thought to be a reasonable speed for a new engine and then changed down to third speed - again at what I thought the right time, this proved to be not so - so down again to second speed, even this was no use, I had to get down to first to get up the hill. Later, after it was run in, I tried it over Sadghyll but slowing down in first, to get round the double bend, it would not pick up speed again and stalled. I did not keep it long.

It was a long time before any other of our pre-war staff returned. John Hayhurst came back to us and Dean Scaife started his own garage at Ambleside. We took on Ralph Armstrong from another part of the country, who settled in Sedbergh and he was with us for many years. He was able to take over such lathe and other machine work from me as, without any training and extremely little experience, I had to take over the management of the business, my father having died just after the war ended.

My father was locking up the garage one evening and hanging up one of the petrol pump hoses, when he had a heart attack. Dr Holliday was called in immediately and diagnosed the condition and said he needed specialist attention and suggested Dr Hay from Windermere. He was telephoned and said, he would come if someone would come for him and later return him. This was agreed but the only car we had available was a Daimler 15, so off I went. It was a filthy night, dark, pouring with rain and blowing a gale. I went as fast as I could, collected Dr Hay and was returning to Kendal via Crook when, descending Crook Brow, the sliding roof blew off completely. I stopped the car, ran back, picked up the roof, jammed it down in position as best I could under the adverse circumstances and for the remainder of the journey I held the roof down with my left hand holding the handle fitting at the leading edge of the roof. I don't remember taking Dr Hay back - but I suppose I must have done.

Father was told that he must have total rest for six weeks. Dr Holliday came in to see him from time to time and when father was told that he could get up on Monday and walk about the bedroom quietly and rest in the chair as much as passible, he was overjoyed. Unfortunately he died at 7am from coronary thrombosis, the day he was due to get up. He was only sixty-six.

The business heretofore had been run entirely by my father and literally I knew nothing at all about this side of it. All the affairs were in father's sole name and there were problems left, right and centre. Mr Leadbeater, manager of the Midland Bank was as helpful as he could be but, when the Inland Revenue started delving into his affairs, they found that an insurance policy had matured just at that time, and could not be paid to any other person and that father had never declared this policy. This found, they went back over his affairs for years, scraping funds off every year for goodness knows how long, the net result was that we had to start trading on a bank overdraft. This at the end of five years slaving our guts out!

We had petrol; we had oil-stocks which were checked at odd intervals by inspectors who did not understand what they were doing, or so it seemed to me. I remember one instance just after the war, when an inspector came round and demanded to dip our petrol tanks. Father took supplies and took what he could get and allocated what tanks it had to go into. I had no idea what we had, it was none of my business and we had seven or eight tanks of varying capacity - taking anything from 500 to 1500 gallons. I thought quickly, "How am I going to get out of this?" I knew which dip rods fitted which tanks. So the 1000 and 1500 gallon tank I used the 500 dip rod on. It couldn't show more than 500 gallons even if it had 1500 gallons. Of course I had to be jolly careful I didn't let it drop out of my hand, for it would have dropped in and been lost completely. So we had hoodwinked the man who came to check on us and he hadn't a clue what he was doing and just took my readings and that was it. It stood us in good stead, we could help a few people without shame at all - it was our petrol - good customers could get a few gallons more than they were entitled to with their ration tickets.

All our large tyre stock - probably in the order of 200-300 tyres of all sizes - were taken over by 'authorised tyre depots', so when we again required tyres for a very tyre-hungry public, we were at a terrific disadvantage. Fortunately our pre-war turnover in tyres was not entirely forgotten and, in spite of a system of permits, we slowly built up a stock and were able to recover a good share of what had been our pre-war tyre business when the tyre manufacturers had been only too eager to supply us with 'parcels of twenty tyres of one size' and 'parcels of 20 tyres of another size', similarly with tubes (now a thing of the past!). Anyone wanting a tyre or tube at this time had to make application on a Government form and wait for a permit, which had then to be submitted to one of the thirteen manufacturers for the order to be executed. Fortunately we had very many customers pre-war who were only too glad to get back to us, amongst them many farmers, doctors and businessmen and some of these had priority for tyre needs. With the permit they were able to place with us, we slowly were able to build up a stock (by putting always a request in for 4 or 5 tyres each time) and again give a service to our customers. Lots of people were willing to say they wanted five tyres when they only needed two. We weren't robbing anybody, we were just building up stock from what had been literally stolen from us. We had to work very hard and conscientiously to get things going again. We got into the tyre business in a big way. The tyre wholesalers came back in a big way, Briggs and one or two from outside. Myers and Bowman at Distington joined hands with us and we bought from them and got a good deal. Then, eventually, big wholesalers took over everywhere.

As a point of interest, I would like to mention that we at Crabtree's received the very first set of five tubeless tyres ever supplied by the Dunlop branch, in Ardwick, Manchester. They had the appearance of being ordinary Dunlop tyres with an inner layer of soft solid rubber lining on the inside, not from bead to bead, but midway down the side walls and across the whole of the tread areas, with a soft thin tapered inner edge to the bead area to make an airtight seal to the rim. The valves supplied with these tyres had soft rubber seal washers both inside and outside the rim and were tightened with a nut and brass washer on the outside. They were fitted by us on to a new Sunbeam Talbot 90 saloon, for Mr W Beck. As a matter of interest the same Mr W Beck bought from us the replica of the Earls Court Show model of the only MGA twin-overhead cam MG we ever supplied. This was very fast indeed but unfortunately did not retain its tune very well and after several attempts we eventually got it 'on song', after a succession of camshaft timing checks, which showed extremely small variation from that laid down by MG. We eventually decided to replace the very long timing chain, which had the immediate effect of restoring its hitherto brilliant performance. Unfortunately, this had to be repeated again six months later in order to restore its power again. Timing of the camshafts was obviously of the greatest importance, which was most unfortunate for the success of this model.

As I have already stated, after WW2 new cars were exceedingly difficult to obtain on the most favourable terms and, in many cases, the manufacturers would have been producing warlike stores of one kind or another (MG were in fact producing aeroplane wings), and a good many would be out of business, due to the massive air raids on Coventry - one of the worst experienced and from which the word 'coventrated' was

Laura my wife making light of untangling the petrol hose

Joe Addy - Croft's mechanic with one of the original Morris Minor's with single ohc.

coined. In fact the Armstrong Siddeley factory was razed to the ground (they were making aero engines) and, on the site next to Armstrong Siddeley, was the factory of Maudsley, which suffered the same fate. They were the manufacturers of heavy goods vehicles and large coach chassis' - they were completely obliterated and never restarted production. Armstrong Siddeley was probably the first manufacturer to present a totally new car to the British market in the form of the Lancaster Six Light Saloon, the Hurricane, a drop head coupé version, and finally, the Typhoon. Production costs escalated to such an extent that it was considered inadvisable to continue with car production, so they teamed up with the Bristol Aeroplane Company and continued in the aircraft industry, as Bristol Siddeley. They also branched into other lines, for example starter batteries for the motor and other users.

John Siddeley became Sir John Siddeley before the war and after Sir Alan Cobham's epic flight to Australia, using Armstrong Siddeley aero engines, I visited the pre-war factory on many occasions and even conducted various clients from Westmorland through the factory, at that time reputed to be one of the cleanest in the industry. Their body shop/despatch department was on another road behind the factory and in the next bay were their radial aero engines - always running.

The aero engines, after completion and first inspection, are started and run at moderate speed for a period, then at a higher and higher speed after certain timed periods. At the end of these test periods, the engines are then totally dismantled and every part thereof is closely scrutinised and, if everything is perfect, it is passed and issued with a test certificate signed by the men responsible for this test. After reassembly it is again tested at maximum permitted speed for a statutory period before release. We must never forget that it was Sir Alan Cobham who made the first non-stop flight to Australia using Armstrong Siddeley radial aero engines, and the first refuelling in the air for the whole journey using Armstrong Siddeley Engines in the refuelling of 'Tanker aircraft' which made it all possible.

As a point of interest, Sir Alan also came to Kendal and offered flights locally at a very reasonable rate and was the first aeroplane ever to land in Kendal. Incidentally when he landed on Spital Field he broke the struts for his undercarriage. He asked someone on the Appleby Road if they could recommend someone who could weld the broken struts - he was directed to Crabtrees in Kirkland. I welded them for him and he offered to give me a flight around the area but I said, "I will only go as far up in an aeroplane, as long as I can keep one foot firmly on the ground!" I didn't go up! (Though have flown quite a lot since!)

Many other factories suffered damage on a lesser scale. I could see this coming as I was now in charge (my brother Bryan was still in Germany). I placed orders with manufacturers with whom, in ordinary circumstances, we would not be doing business. I cannot recall them all now but for certain our list included Allard, Healey, Ford, Hillman & Humber, Riley, Rover, Standard, Morris Commercial vans (a local man ordered one of these and when he got it offered me £100 in cash, as a thank you, which I did not accept) HRG, Rolls Royce, Renault, Morris and MG - of them all, the only one we represented were Rootes Group and Armstrong Siddeley, they let us have a Hurricane fairly quickly followed by a Lancaster a bit later. In fact we ordered whatever cars we thought we would be able to sell. At one period we had a waiting list for more than two hundred Hillman cars alone.

Mr and Mrs Bateman, besides having the Bateman Motor Museum at Coniston, took over Wilsons Garage at Lindale and the Rootes dealership, involving Hillman, Humber, Sunbeam and Singer cars. Mr Bateman also took on BMW cars and made a real impact with this make. Our two firms in Lindale and Kendal worked very well together, if either of us required one of the wide range of Rootes cars and had not the car in stock (there were far too many models for this to be an economic possibility), we first telephoned each other to ascertain whether they had the required car in stock and if they had, then would they release it to the other, which usually they did and at the same time probably another model was expected in return, with a cash adjustment. This understandably widened the range of cars we were able to offer 'ex-stock'.

The Batemans must have had a large amount of money tied up in their museum for they had a vast quantity of cars - the smallest being a BMW Isetta (early post war), including Rolls Royce, Bentley, Jaguar, Riley, Austin, Morris, Standard, Ford, Sunbeam Rapier, Sunbeam, Sunbeam Tiger, a selection of Hillman models, plus a representative range of other makes.

The first Rolls Royce we sold which was ordered through SMT, Carlisle, was refused by the client when it arrived. We had another name on our list against this car and we offered it to him, he also refused it, so it went up on to the newly installed first floor and was sheeted up. In the meantime Mr Leadbeater was getting hot under the collar about the rising overdraft we were running and telephoned about once every week to see if we had sold it. He pressed us to return it and I am sure SMT (Scottish Motor Traction) would have willingly taken it back because there were literally no cars available in a market going mad for cars, so that by now a black market had opened up. I told Mr Leadbeater that we were unwilling to return it as costs had arisen which only a retail sale could clear, not least of course being the bank overdraft charges. Short of terminating our overdraft facility, there was little he could do about it. We eventually sold the car at full list price to a fish and chip proprietor. As things turned out the purchaser got a bargain - a Rolls Royce for £5,585 - compare that with today's prices! One cannot buy a mini for that today!

The next similar incident was with an Armstrong Siddeley Lancaster saloon. The person who ordered this car, because of the delay, cancelled the order, so that when we were advised to collect the car and we had another valued client who did lots of business with us, wanting a new car, I explained the position to him and he said, "Well, offer it to this chap again, but in the meantime I will complete a set of taxation forms so that you can tax it in my name, if he refuses delivery still." We did just that and I took the car to the original client's house on trade plates and he was quite forthright saying, "I don't want the car and you know I cancelled the order." I said, "Is that your last word?" He then said, "Of course it is!" So I bid him good morning. On the way back, I called in the motor taxation office and taxed the car in the name of my other client, again at list price (although I had already had an offer of £300 over the top in cash, if I would sell it to yet another person). This kind of thing went on for a long time, when cars were in short supply and I can honestly say, that we never took any part in this dishonest trade, either before or after the SMMT (Society of Motoring Manufacture and Trader) introduced the Covenant Scheme to curb the practice, on pain of severe penalties, although this did not eradicate it totally.

I know of one certain trader who propositioned an acquaintance on these lines, "We will tax and insure a new car in your name on these conditions. It will cost you nothing but the petrol you use. You may only use it on fine Sundays. You are to keep the floor carpets covered with the mats we will put in the car. No children in the car. It is to be always locked up in your garage when not in use. You will be expected to care for the car as if it were your own. We know you are a good and careful driver and the maximum mileage you are permitted will be 2,000 (two thousand). The car is to be presented to us for its 500 miles service at the appropriate time and the car to be returned to us on or before the end of the three months. There will be no charge to you and we may possibly renew your contract."

Signed owner   date   Dealer

Signed user   date

The length of the contract coincided with the SMMT Covenant period. The contract I know was repeated later with another new car.

To try to alleviate the severe car shortage problem, several makers rehashed their pre-war models - not so Jowett, the Yorkshire firm based at Idle, Bradford. Pre-war they had made reliable and robust cars and light vans with twin cylinder, horizontally opposed, water-cooled, side valve engines. These cars were not expected to go fast but at least they were utterly reliable and after the war they aspired to tackle a more advanced market with the four cylinder, horizontally opposed, ohv, water-cooled engine, which sported the (unusual at that time) hydraulic tappets for their push rod operated valve gear. These cars were good and reliable and also - as distinct from previous Jowetts - good performers but, unfortunately, they had an achilles heel - the location of the sparking plugs, which were fitted vertically into depressions in the water jacketed, cylinder heads. They could not stand external water and, whilst I am not suggesting that ordinary rainfall was a problem, they would not tolerate any water standing on the surface of the road. We found, in our situation as motor agents and repairers in the years following the introduction of the Jowett Javelin, that our first call-out to a waterlogged engine was always a Jowett Javelin. The reason being, about three miles south of our premises at Grate Farm, there was an ordinary small stream with a limited collection area which, in the case of heavy rain always exceeded the capacity of the culvert, which took the water across the road. The result was that the water which could not go under the A6 road simply went over the road surface and continued on its way to the River Kent. The water on the road was never deep because the road was fairly level but it was quite wide. Most vehicles were unaffected but, due to the unusual design of the Javelin, it was badly affected. The depressions in which the spark plugs were fitted filled with water and caused complete and sudden stoppage. I have no knowledge of this phenomenon ever having been resolved by Jowett cars but they had other far more serious problems to deal with as a company. This may be out of context but you may wonder why Jowett cars are no longer with us - indeed many readers may never have heard the name of Jowett cars.

The bodies for the Javelin were made for them by Briggs Motor Bodies and were of all steel construction and very modern in appearance, whereas all previous Jowett bodies had been coachbuilt on wooden frames.

All went well at first but, as production of the Javelin increased, so they required more bodies. Unfortunately for Jowett, Ford also used Briggs Bodies and, as the variety of models and the demand for more bodies for Ford (who largely owned Briggs) increased, so Jowett had no chance of surviving such a squeeze. The only other body manufacturer of any size was also fully committed and could not entertain the tooling up required. So unfortunately Jowett died.

My father used a Jowett Weasel for a few years, this was a pre-1939-45 war production model and consisted of the horizontally opposed, twin cylinder engine and a coach built, four-seater, touring-type body, with hood. It was also fitted with two carburetters and a close ratio gearbox - which incidentally was a delight to use. Unfortunately, the increase in actual power delivered to the wheels was minimal, although it was nice enough to handle.

After the war, amongst other cars we had ordered, were Renault and Citroen - though they were never received. We did however later in 1947-8 sell a few Renaults, including the Quatre Chevaux, the Dauphine and the 2 litre Fregate, all of which gave good service. I even visited the Renault factory at Billancourt, which at the time was probably the most advanced motor factory in Europe - the previous factory having been decimated by the RAF. There, for the first time, I saw the all-steel bodies being produced. There were cables and clamps everywhere and, by simply throwing one large switch, the whole body was spot welded together in its jigs. I also watched the first transfer machine I had ever seen - it was difficult to believe what was being done. A whole cylinder block was picked up off the floor after being completely de-sanded and, when it had passed from station to station and rigidly clamped at every stage, a finished cylinder block was removed at the far end.

Some years later, when there was still a famine for new cars, we took up an area dealership for OEC, which were made in Portsmouth. Deliveries were very erratic, perhaps because the rail fare for the long journey was prohibitive, which would of course help them to decide to deliver the bulk of their output more locally and there must have been many motorcycle dealers much nearer to hand.

We later took on DMW and we sold a lot of these motorcylces. Sometimes we had as many as a dozen in stock and upon application, we appointed Midland Garage, at Lancaster, as sub-dealers because they complained that they were not getting a fair crack of the whip from the Lancaster dealers. The DMW was unique at that time, the frame was made from square steel tubing throughout and all the pieces were assembled in a strong steel jig and rigidly clamped - they then had all the joints welded at one setting. They generally fitted Villiers engines but there was also a French four-stroke engine available at a price, which had a single overhead camshaft. These were too expensive for the average buyer which resulted in us only selling one of these. On one occasion

197 DMW Villiers engine. Albion provided the gears for the Villiers gearbox. One of the first motorbikes to be fitted with a square frame.

Laura and I visited their modern factory in Clermont-Ferrand in central France. The brains behind this set up were two French engineers who had been fighter pilots in WW2. They designed all their production machines plus design and machining of all the components.

I know from previous experience that motorcycles and cars do not mix - a motorcyclist is likely to come into a garage and lean his machine against the nearest car and, with paintwork being so easily marked and even the panel dented, it is 'not on'. However, we changed our policy to include motorcycles in 1950-55 and sold quite a lot, we even tuned one OEC which won many events.

In the late 1940s, as I said, we had moved house to Oxenholme. On one Saturday in midsummer, before the M6 existed, the traffic on the A65 into Kendal stretched for two and a half miles and was taking forty minutes to pass through. This particular day, I could not even get into the traffic queue to return to work, the cars were literally quite bumper to bumper. So I walked across the road to speak to a driver of one of the cars and asked him where he was going and he said, "Carlisle!" So I went to the car immediately behind him and ascertained that he was going into the Lake District. I told him that I could lead them to Kendal

Official opening of Kendal Motors Ltd - March 1956. I presented Alderman W F Pennington with an inscribed silver pencil immediately after the ceremony.

photo courtesy of The Westmorland Gazette

Introduction day for the new Hillman Imp in Kendal. From the left: Laura Crabtree, W Fulton Pennington, Bernard Crabtree, Bryan Crabtree, F Wheatley Knowles, The tall man with papers in his left hand is Inspector Foxcroft, Cumberland & Westmorland Police. 1968

photo courtesy of The Westmorland Gazette

avoiding all the traffic and the car in front had agreed to let me into the traffic ahead of him and I would lead. I said, "If you want to pass the message back to the next car behind and ask him to do the same, then we would all be at the north end of Kendal in about six minutes." The traffic behind was solid right back to Crooklands and beyond, so when the cars in front moved forward for three car lengths, the driver of the car I had first approached allowed me in, in fifty yards we turned right into Oxenholme village, right through the village and up the hill as far as the Station Inn, where we turned left until we reached the Sedbergh Road. We turned left again and skirted round the east side of Kendal to the Appleby Road. I told the Carlisle driver to turn right at the Duke of Cumberland and gave the car going to the Lakes the directions through town. They had all saved about half an hour and there was a queue of cars behind similarly taking this short cut. How valuable local knowledge can be!

One of the worst incidents that occurred during my lifetime at the garage (51 years) was the tragic accident, which involved our best mechanic and Captain Maple's wife. Captain Maples ran a 'Y' type MG saloon, but his wife drove a Renault 4. Our mechanic was out testing a Sunbeam Rapier he had been tuning and adjusting for a client who lived and worked as a Police Officer, in London, (her brother-in-law was our salesman, Joss Smith, and he and his wife Nora were resident in our district - actually Selside).

He was testing this Rapier and admits he was travelling at more than 70mph, when he saw an old lady in her Renault 4 coming down the hill off the Crook Road, where it joins the main Kendal/Windermere road, about a couple of miles out of Kendal. Our mechanic saw what was happening and began to slow, in order to let the lady and her car out into the road towards Kendal. He then saw the Renault stop at the junction and assumed that she had seen him and was allowing him to pass in front of her. This, however, turned out not to be the case. He began to accelerate the Sunbeam again and had almost reached the junction, when the Renault shot forward. It was not possible to stop the Rapier in the short distance between the two cars - he collided with the front end of the rear-engined car and it was very badly damaged and the body deformed, allowing the rear hinged front door to fly open, whereupon the old lady fell out onto the road, as a result she was badly concussed and died in hospital later that evening.

My family during this time had been growing up fast. Both had done well at school - Christine had gone to the Girls' High School and later Fairfield at Ambleside, and gone on to hold down good jobs in secretarial work. Peter won a scholarship and went on to Heversham Grammar School - from there he went on an apprenticeship course at Morris Commercial Cars Limited at Adderley Park, Birmingham. At that time they were manufacturing vehicles from ten hundred weight to seven tons, including Ambulance chassis of which we sold a number to the local Ambulance Department.

Flood in 1954 at it's height was four inches on top of the Romney footbridge.

photo courtesy of The Westmorland Gazette

View of the torrent racing down Lound Road when the bridge arches could take no more water. The water came into the garage but only affected one of the petrol tanks.

photo courtesy of The Westmorland Gazette

CAR COLLECTION
- (EX-FACTORY) AND
MEMORABLE 'CALL-OUTS'

We used to collect our own cars from the factories before the large car transporters came into being. These huge vehicles, sometimes with two-deck trailers, offered the rapid clearance the various factories required. The transport drivers put the cars on the various deck levels, in such order as they were to deliver, according to the destination of each car. These delivery charges were added to the car invoice and were not unreasonably high - in any case we, the dealers, had no option. For our part the collecting of single cars could be a bit of a nuisance when we were very busy or if we were short staffed for any reason - holidays, sickness and pressure of work in the garage and here are some of my own experiences of car collection over the years.

My first car collection was a four cylinder, 12hp, AC, two seater from the factory at Thames Ditton. This was during the largest general strike ever known in England, in 1926. The rail service was badly disrupted but I caught the 7.15am train from Oxenholme, the train I was to take on many such journeys. Very few trains were running and it took one longer to get to the factory by train than it did the return journey by car. The maximum speed we always held, when driving new cars, was 30mph and me being only seventeen years old, with little driving experience, although competent, the return journey took twelve hours.

There were no problems with the car but parts of the return journey through Staffordshire and Lancashire were through 'hostile territory'. First through crowds of pottery workers demonstrating in the streets and, further north, through the towns in the Lancashire coalfields. Whilst neither I nor the car suffered material damage, it was a most unnerving experience, driving through crowds of demonstrating workers and it was generally a case of proceeding slowly and in first gear, to avoid being the cause of an 'incident'.

The AC was ordered by Mr John Coward, an employee of the Midland Bank. It was a very pretty car and it ran well. It was fitted with AC's own four cylinder, water-cooled, side-valve engine, which was, I was reliably informed, a copy of the British Anzani engine, it had replaced about a year previously. The list price of the car was £333 and it was guaranteed for three years. No claims under guarantee were ever made, nor were there any problems with the car - it was very reliable. Mr Coward was married three years later and soon found it necessary to sell the car to our firm (I actually bought it myself) in order to provide for his family. The bank moved him away from Kendal about this time to another branch.

The next vehicle I collected was a 3-4 ton Berliet lorry chassis with solid tyres all round. No mudguards, no lamps, no windscreen, not even a cushion to sit on. A box-like structure had been put over the petrol tank, upon which I sat. It was November and days were short and it took me three days to bring it from Richmond, in Surrey, and what a journey! I got as far as Dunstable, where it got dark and I could go no further. I parked in a garage forecourt and found digs for the night. In the morning, I was up and away at 8.30am when it became light enough to see. I had not gone very far, when a car overtook me and told me one of the two large boxes had fallen off. So I went back and found that the other one was also about to fall off! Almost all vehicles, (certainly at that time, there have been modifications in the car world since then), had channel section frame members and crossmembers.

The two large boxes contained a five lamp lighting set, batteries (the chassis had magneto ignition), tools, brackets for the mudguards and an electric horn, but no horn was fitted as there was nothing electrical on the chassis except the magneto.

Two timbers about 3" x 1" had been fitted between the chassis side-members and nailed upwards, with the boxes thus securing them to the chassis. This might have sufficed for a ten or fifteen mile journey but from Richmond in Surrey, some two hundred and eighty miles and with a solid-tyred vehicle, it was totally unrealistic to expect them to remain in this position over the rear axle when, for half its time, the back end was airborn! So this was another problem, apart from my backside which was feeling the effects of sitting on plain boards with gaps between them, on a vehicle which spent half its time with its wheels in the air.

I must have had to pick these two boxes up off the road another half dozen times, in spite of me having positioned the nails in different positions, to get a better grip in the wood. By the time I reached Stoke-on-Trent, I had had enough and when I saw an agricultural suppliers shop, in I went and bought the only kinds of rope he stocked - these were about twenty feet long (each) and were the ones used by farmers for breaking in horses. I put both these boxes on the seat beside me, fortunately with it being over the petrol tank the space was very long, so there was room for them both.

It was almost dark when I got through Warrington and I could find no place to park - so I did the only thing I could, I went on and when I got to Ashton-in-Makerfield, it was totally dark, so I pulled on to a garage forecourt and left it there for the night. I went across the road to a pub and asked if I could stay the night. They made me a meal and I had a bed for the night - I was away before 8.30 in the morning and the garage was still closed.

I must have thought I was in heaven because I had no further trouble until descending the hill into Walton-le-Dale, south of Preston, when the seat collapsed! I descended the hill almost to the bottom and pulled on to the forecourt of a garage there and explained my predicament. Fortunately, they had timber and more nails and were able to put the seat back, substantially reinforced. It got me back without further incident. I had got as far as Levens Bridge, when I met a man on a Rover motor-cycle going south. When he saw me he turned round and told me to pull over, which I did." His next words, "Where the hell have you been? You've taken three days to collect a vehicle!" To which I replied, "You don't know the half of it!" He went on, "Your father has sent me to look for you!" I had explaining to do of course when I arrived but I was still only seventeen and the same would have happened to whoever had been collecting the chassis.

I remember collecting a two litre Sunbeam Talbot from Ryton-on-Dunsmore, just outside Coventry and, as cars were almost unavailable at that time, I went via Donald Healey's factory to see if I could prize out one or two of his new models, as I had time to spare. He let me have one, which I drove from Kendal to Stainton, near Blackpool, where a firm had arranged to build a body for us. Not wishing to take another man off his work, (we were still short handed after the war), and being a fine day, I strapped my new Douglas motorcycle to the back of the temporary seat. I got to Blackpool alright but no sooner had I got the bike off the Healey chassis, than it began to rain and so I set off for Kendal some fifty miles away, totally unsuitably clothed. The rain became a torrent, I got back soaked to the skin but was at work as usual next morning. A hot bath is a wonderful thing after a soaking!

Whilst I was at the Healey works, I realised our garage in Kendal had more floor space and had far more equipment. All they were doing was assembling a lot of parts bought in, in fact everything that goes to make up a car chassis - there were no bodies of any kind on site. I suppose that was the reason he let me buy one of his completed chassis. He was an outspoken critic of the two litre Sunbeam - especially the hood. But that was 1946 and there had been a war!

Mr C E M Hodding took a farm at Lowgill for the rearing of poultry, and presumably the sale of eggs and birds for the table. He was courting and then married a lady from Burton-in-Kendal. They went to the Motor Show whilst on honeymoon and chose the car they would like. He already had a four cylinder American Durant, which would have to be sold of course. Mr Hodding was the only driver and they had no accommodation for two cars at Lowgill and, in any case, Lowgill is no place to leave a car outside in winter time.

At the car show they had, of course, plenty to choose from and together they decided upon a Grand Prix model French Salmson and they gave my father the brochure they had obtained from the attendant on the stand at Olympia (in those days).

I read a brochure at the Motor Show which explained the car. The Salmson had a four cylinder, dohc (double overhead camshaft) engine - truly a rarity in those days. It also had four wheel brakes; not all cars were so equipped with these at that time. This system was unique as far as I recollect, in that the foot brakes worked on only three of the wheels and the handbrake on the fourth. I digested all this information which was to stand me in good stead when I was detailed to collect this car from a warehouse (it turned out to be) in south west London. I think I was probably just as interested in the car, as was the purchaser, which again was a good thing. In those days, when I went to collect a new car, whatever its specification I had only one aim in mind - get it back to Kendal safely, as soon as possible, having the strict instruction placed of course not to exceed 30mph ever!

I got to the Salmson warehouse, near London, about 5.15pm and found them about to lock up. I told them I had been told to get the car back as soon as possible and that I was to travel overnight to accomplish this.

They grudgingly reopened the half closed door and went to bring the car down. They had to push start it because the battery was flat. I very soon found myself in a bit of a quandary, here was I in a district I did not know, a long way from any principal roads leading north, in rush hour traffic and with a flat battery, which involved me keeping the rev counter needle on 2,000 to prevent it stalling. I managed but, always a thinker, I was trying to decide a firm method of getting home without trouble of any kind and I formulated a plan I thought to be workable. I remembered that at Newcastle-under-Lyme there was a big car park in the middle of the town that sloped down with the road and I thought I must get on to that park towards the top end and stay in the car all night - it would run down the slope and I would thus be able to start it when I wanted to leave.

It did not work out quite like that, here was I with only two forays of experience and with a car whose lights went dim every time I slowed down. However I had been that way before and was looking out for a sharp left hand turn with a fire station round the corner. Traffic was such that I had to slow down a number of times and I must have passed the turn, I proceeded about half a mile and there was a canal bridge in front of me which I did not remember, so I reversed down on to the towpath but unfortunately got my right rear wheel over the edge of the canal. This upset me but, as I have already said, I am a thinker. I was only too conscious of the lights problem and kept the engine running whilst I thought. My mind went back to the Salmson brochure I had read. I still kept the engine running over 1000 to maintain the state of the battery and I remembered the paragraph about the foot brake operating on the nearside wheel only and also that the car had a solid rear axle (no differential, so that effectively both rear wheels were brake locked). I speeded up the engine and let in the clutch in first gear, gently releasing the handbrake at the same time to avoid stalling the engine. The car pulled itself from the impossible position, to four wheels on the towpath. I proceeded to the car park I referred to previously and parked so that I could get a bit of sleep. I returned safely to Kendal through judicious use of the lighting switch.

A 15hp Armstrong Siddeley, six cylinder, side valve saloon, with black fabric covered roof, was the first we brought from the factory and it looked very smart - all black with just one red 'coach line'. It did not have a self-changing gearbox on this model but a very noisy 'crank' box which, when reaching top gear, was dead silent - both engine and gearbox.

I must have travelled fifty miles from Coventry when the engine stopped and, from the experience I had gained in the servicing of all kinds of cars, immediately knew it was a petrol supply problem. The fuel tank at that time was in the scuttle panel, with the filler cap under the bonnet. I opened the nearside of the bonnet and turned the petrol tap off, then I removed the petrol filter bowl, which was full of residue. We wrote to Armstrong Siddeley the next day to inform them of the trouble experienced and they sent a new fuel tank with compliments and regretting the trouble caused. No further troubles were experienced then or in the future. Incidentally, in those days, cars came with a full tool kit!

We sent our usual driver to Coventry to collect a new Hillman saloon but he later telephoned us from Litchfield to inform us that there was something wrong with the back axle - he said, "It is very hot!" We told him to telephone the factory and gave him the number and that they were to take him to Coventry with them and we would collect him the following day. John Airey from Lakeland Garage, in Windermere, happened to be in our garage at the time and I told him of the predicament. He said, "I am going down to Birmingham and taking Colin to bring a new Reliant back with me!" I then told him that two of us were going, one to collect a Morris Commercial van at Adderley Park, Birmingham and the other to collect a Hillman, from Coventry. He said that he would take us all. I was a bit doubtful, he was taking us in a Reliant Robin and I expressed my doubts but he said he often had four in! I will say no more than, it was an 'experience'!

Back to our Hillman, the axle had never had any oil in it. The only vehicle we ever collected without oil. The whole axle unit was replaced and no charges were made by Hillman of course.

On another occasion, I was going to collect a Commer, eight hundredweight van and offered to take Laura with me. On that day something must have gone wrong with British Rail, instead of arriving in Coventry at 1.05pm we arrived at 11.45am, the only time in hundreds of journeys that this happened. We were actually in Ryton before the factory stopped for lunch and I had got the van before lunch but I could not drive it out of the compound as it failed to get petrol through. They took it into a repairs department, diagnosed petrol pump failure and fitted another new one. It seemed okay, so we drove it out of the compound, stopped at Martins Garage and bought sufficient petrol to get us home. We left there and got on to the Coventry by-pass and I felt the car slowing up, I glanced into the mirror and saw a Jaguar coming up behind and a Police car chasing him. I could see that with my engine slowing up and probably going to stop, I was likely to be rammed from behind by either the Jag or the Police car, so I switched suddenly on to the wide grass verge on my nearside. The Police car hadn't a hope in hell of catching the Jag - so he switched to an easier prey - me! Unfortunately, he was out of luck, I knew as much about the law as he did and I complied with the law in every detail.

First of all, he wanted to know what I was playing at going on to the verge like that, to which I replied, "My engine was stalling and I did not want either the Jag that you were chasing or you at your top speed into my back, so I did the only thing possible with a dying engine, got out of the road of both of you." I then went on to tell him of my problem with this van since I collected it. By this time the Jag was miles away, although I suppose he had got the registration number. Now follows the Police procedure. "You know you are not permitted passengers on LTP (Limited Trade Plates - cost £5) unless you have an authority signed by an official of the firm you work for, have you got one?" I produced the chit, he looked at it and then went to take particulars of the licence, they were identical. Next he said, "Who is the young lady with you?" I said, "My wife!" He then asked for Laura's identification and fortunately she had her driving licence with her. Thus satisfied that we were not breaking the law in any way, I asked him if he could tell me of a garage who would come and fix the car, as I needed to get back to Kendal that night. He very graciously took me to the garage and, being downhill, I was able to drive it there - just!

He introduced me to the owner of the garage and I briefly explained the problem, including the replaced petrol pump. He put the car on the lift and disconnected the fuel line from the bottom front face of the tank but nothing came out so he then got a $\frac{1}{16}$" diameter welding rod and pushed it into the tank and of course a jet of petrol came out. He immediately stopped this by reconnecting the pipe. He then said, "I can't do anything more for you tonight, we are just closing." I said, "If you will sell me that spanner and that length of welding rod, I will pay you for your labour and for these two items. I will then be able to deal with it on the road if it occurs again." He did just that and I tipped him for his help. We got home but instead of being home by 8pm it was 1am. We wrote to Hillman at Ryton and told them the whole story and they sent a cheque for our out-of-pocket expenses and for later fitting a new petrol tank, which they sent on. If it had not been replaced, it would have been a continuous source of trouble.

So the above incidents are the problems I incurred over the period of collecting our own cars from 1922 to the 1960s when transporters took over - not bad!

Now call-outs were jobs I went to after hours. Generally on such journeys I was alone with the breakdown truck, a twenty-five hundredweight Commer van, with crane, breakdown ambulance etc. I went to a call-out in 1925, to a Rover 12 with a collapsed wheel - at least that was the message and it was at Shap summit. When I arrived, I discovered a car with only one wheel out of the five that was serviceable, and that was not the spare wheel. The car was proceeding south towards Kendal when the nearside front tyre burst, the car swerved into the rock face at this point and the result was a collapse of the nearside front wire wheel. The driver somehow managed to get the car pulled away from the rock face and it immediately crossed the road and skidded sideways, collapsing the two offside wheels. I just stood and gaped! I had a good look round the car and underneath and I saw a possibility. On that model Rover (late pre-war), there was a heavy tubular cross-member amidships. I had the demented idea, that I might manage to lift it and tow it in. I got hold of the front end by both front springs and lifted the front end to about maximum height, then I manoeuvred the two-wheeled ambulance, right under the middle of the car and chained it to the ambulance. The front end was then in the air, so I then dragged the front end down until the centre of the front axle was resting on the telescopic towing pole, which was then secured to the towing bracket, at the rear of our vehicle. Both front springs and the front axle were then chained to the towing pole. Here, we have a prime subject for a road accident! A car balanced, one could almost say, pivoted on two substantial crotches, under the approximate middle of the car and chained to the towing pole. One good pot hole or a very little too much speed, nothing over 10mph and the whole lot would have toppled over with disastrous results! It was delivered into the garage no worse for the experience and it was only my nerves that were a little frayed!

On another occasion, we were informed that Shap was blocked with snow and, being a bit of a motorcyclist, I thought I would like to go and see what was going on. I had my new 500cc OEC Blackburne, with competition tyres, so I did not expect to have any trouble with traction, so I got decked up in my all weather gear and, by travelling on the virgin snow at the roadside, had no trouble getting right to the top of Hucks Brow. I had stopped on the way up to look around but was determined to get to the top, where I leaned the bike against the rock face on the east side of the road. A chap came to me and asked what conditions were like further down there, I could only tell him that traffic of all types was stuck in every possible position. He was dead scared and he asked me if I could drive a car and when I told him I could, he asked if I would drive the car down there for him. This was something of a challenge, which I accepted.

It was 1928 and the car was a large 15hp Citroen. The owner thankfully handed the wheel over to me and he crowded into the car with his wife and family. Conscious of the responsibility I had rather foolishly taken upon myself, I started the engine, engaged first gear and determined not to let it get a 'slide on', just allowed it to crawl along threading our way between stranded vehicles. It looked like hundreds of cars and lorries scattered unevenly all down the hill. We eventually arrived safely at the bottom of Hucks Brow and proceeded just far enough beyond to be quite clear of the traffic. He thanked me profusely, that was all I expected - and indeed all I got - plus the experience.

One thing I had totally overlooked was the mile long uphill trek I had to undertake in my heaviest motorcycling gear to collect my OEC. Talk about sweating - I could not have had a heavier sweat in a Turkish bath! I got home safely without 'dropping the bike' even once. It was an experience - one I have no wish to repeat

One of the worst accidents in Kendal we were called out to, was soon after the 1939-45 war, in Kirkland, adjacent to Nether Bridge. A heavy lorry with twin-wheels on both driven rear axles was proceeding southwards down the A6, when a motorcycle coming off the A65 over Nether Bridge, who probably did not know the road and was travelling far too quickly, ran slap into the side of the lorry and went between the wheels on the nearside of the two rear axles. It was too horrible to contemplate. The motorcyclist was killed. Fortunately we were taken off the job by the Fire Service Rescue Team. I don't really think we could have dealt with it.

Immediate post first war trial lined up for the start. Kit Parker 2nd motorcycle from left on front row. R M (Dicky) Chaplow next to his wife on left.

Mrs Elizabeth Chaplow ('Auntie' to her friends) on a two-stroke, two-speed, all chain drive Velocette - but without clutch!

The Westmorland
Motor Club

I am a past president of the Westmorland Motor Club and now a life member. One of the few who succeeded in breathing new life into the club, with energetic work in preparing a case for the resuscitation of this old club and by arousing the interest of the 'next generation' of motor-cyclists and car owners.

I think the last event run by the then club, was held on Bank Head (on the hill going over between Kendal and Underbarrow), these were riders competing from the principal motorcycle manufacturers in 1925. This was run on closed roads (one of which was Orton Scar), though this facility was later stopped. Although I was unable to be present because I was busy at work, I could hear them with their open exhausts, right down in Kirkland. I wanted to go but could not get permission because we were busily engaged in getting the three year old garage business running on a sound foundation.

I am not aware of all the reasons for leaving Orton Scar as this, being so much longer, would have been more spectacular but probably the accidental death in 1919-20 of Guy Jefferies had much to do with it. That day, Guy Jefferies, on completion of the first runs at Orton Scar on his Norton, was the fastest but when, after the second run, the hill was ascended by a works rider on a factory machine (a similar Norton) in a shorter time, Guy was not going to be beaten on his home ground and was making a very fast climb, when he ran into a telegraph pole and was killed. The Guy Jefferies Memorial Trophy was later presented to the club by the family in his memory. This was to be competed for annually and was to be presented to the person gaining most points in all competitions, based upon three points for a win, two for second and one for a third place. Years later, I was to win that award in the car section three times in the 1930s. If there was a tie in the number of the points for the award, it was held six months by each of the winners. On one occasion the same number of points were held by W H Milburn (BSA motorcycle) and myself (MG car) for six months each.

These are some of the very early and original members as have been related to me over the years in addition to those mentioned below-though not complete - Bryan Jefferies, Guy Jefferies, W Montgomery, Arthur Moffat, Bert Hill, Bert Turner, W Weatherburn. My father, L S (Kit) Parker, William Hutchinson, R M Chaplow, Thomas Chaplow, Louis Handley and Freddy Brennand were all members of the club when it went into abeyance.

Being now the oldest living member of the club, I am often asked why the club closed down for a couple of years, until Harry Skirrow (definitely the prime mover) came to see me at work, to see if I thought the club could be got going again. I talked it over with my father and asked why the club had ceased to operate and I was given full chapter and verse.

The story was told to me in these terms: that after WW1 the young soldiers, having been demobbed, were returning home after their disastrous experiences in the army, relatively quickly they began to get back into civilian life. Some had left treasured bikes and cars behind when they joined up and proceeded to get them out and into some kind of running order - new machines obviously were not available immediately! Another diversion besides the bikes (and the odd car or two) was the fact that these young men were finding female company after a long absence and a good many began, after relatively short periods of courtship, with weddings not too long after.

During this period, they had been going for runs on their bikes and the Westmorland Motor Club, founded in 1910, became alive again and of course competitions were arranged. Other things were going on at the same time and babies began to be born, first at a trickle, then as something rather more daunting. By the time the 1925 Hill Climb had been organised and run, maternal pressures were being imposed on the new husbands and fathers to spend not so much time with the motorcycle and the old cars but to devote more time to the wife and family. As a consequence, there was a very rapid decline in the number of entries for competitions arranged and there may also have been financial pressure and all of which caused the club to go into abeyance. All the trophies were put in a locked tin trunk, including Louis Handley's timing gear and other sundry items of equipment, in what was then Martin's Bank and the cash in hand was left on deposit, under the trusteeship of the Bank, with certain nominated club members to have access to the contents. Similarly there was a multiplicity in the number of signatures they required to withdraw any of the capital deposited.

Throughout 1927 Harry Skirrow, Bob Elliot, Ron Mason and myself had been 'recruiting' known members of the last operative committee who required of us 'new boys', assurances, a sort of guarantee, that we

Kit Partker on the left and John Rigg, both on Scott motorcycles about 1927.

Pre 1921. On the left is Guy Jeffreys, Billy Westwood on his Triumph and Bryan Jeffreys. Both the Jeffreys on Nortons.

Bernard on his 500cc ohv OEC Blackburne racing up Helm - just took 46 seconds from bottom of Helm near to A65, to the top near the ordnance survey point.

Bernard on top of Helm with Tommy Chaplow on 500cc, AJS, in 1928.

would be responsible for the funds and the trophies and, as back-up to this, they also needed to know how many prospective members we had and a list of their names and addresses in order to verify our statements. Literally every moment of spare time was used in making these preparations. No records were ever made of what we did, where we went, or what we spent, which incidentally was all out of our own pockets.

It soon became evident that I would require a 'decent bike', so I bought, as already mentioned, from my father, a New Gerrard 350cc, ohv, Blackburne, with three-speed, wide ratio gearbox, which I thought would be very suitable. Unfortunately, I did not realise just what lay ahead. It had only 2½ inches ground clearance under the outside flywheel and this took a lot of punishment in the years ahead. The dents in the flywheel rim were permanent proof for which the Kentmere side of Garburn was largely responsible. I made a distance piece to fit on the top end of the Webb fork spring, although this lifted the steering head by about one inch, it made little difference to the flywheel clearance.

During that year, Garburn was to see us every Sunday and we encouraged one or two like-minded chaps to come along with us - Ronnie Mason, Bob Elliot and Tom Taylor were amongst the first. We all had standard machines with works silencers, so we were not committing a noise nuisance. We were a new generation of wartime schoolboys and were regularly going over Garburn Pass both from the Kentmere side and the Troutbeck side, also over Gatesgarth Pass into Mardale (it had not been flooded in those days).

During this time, amongst the shrewd moves we made, was to get the backing of a few of the previous members, which included L S (Kit) Parker, Bert Hill, Bert Turner, R M (Dicky) Chaplow, W H Hutchinson, Arthur J Miles, Cuthbert Whiteside and my father Zenas Crabtree. We had also asked Harold B Wakefield if he would be president and, after due consideration, he agreed to accept the office. With this list, I was delegated to see R M Chaplow, a man small in stature but large in experience and influence. He put rather a lot of conditions to us, to which we agreed in principle and we got permission, on presenting a list of twenty would-be members, to proceed and the club was restarted. A General Meeting was held at the County Hotel, which had previously been the Club's headquarters, then run by Jimmy Dougal.

Dicky Chaplow proposed that Louis Handley should be invited to rejoin, together with Fred Brennand and John Hall, so at least we were guided by these 'old timers'. The amount of the subscription was decided upon, 7/6 (37½p) per annum, entry in trials to be 1/6 (7½p). The first event was a social run held at Easter 1928 and there was a good turn

135

out of cars and bikes - my new 500cc, overhead valve, OEC Blackburne, being one. On the whole, it was a very satisfactory road machine and its road performance was exemplary. It was very modern in every respect, in fact a great deal more modern than many, with interchangeable wheels and brakes and the very latest Blackburne engine, with inside flywheels etc and a fully duplex cradle frame, also a guaranteed top speed of 100 mph (in 1928), which was faster than a 'Cammy' Norton of that time, not that I wanted so much speed. I remember on one occasion, when Laura was on the pillion, we climbed Kirkstone from the Patterdale side, the speed not dropping below 55mph at any time. That was in 1928 and in top gear!

In 1928 we had been to a most unusual motorcycling event on a stretch of old grass grown Roman Road, almost never used except perhaps by agriculturists. Len Ellwood, a well-known local motorcycle mechanic, had built up an old machine with very eccentric wheels on purpose - it was worse than riding a horse (say I, who has never been astride a horse!). The event was to ride the machine between two clearly marked lines, about two hundred yards apart, which sounds not too difficult; but with wheels of differing diameter, one 24", the other 26", the jumps are out of sequence and unpredictable and it was rather frightening to ride at any speed.

The event over, we all returned to the Grayrigg main road and sat astride our machines till all had gathered at this point. Harry Greenbank on his 500cc Model E Ariel, Jack Robinson on his 500cc BSA Sloper, Henry Sutton on his 350cc, ohv, AJS, Fred Remington on his 350cc, ohc, Velocette and Gilbert Parkinson on a 350cc, ohv, New Imperial. Henry Sutton, Fred Remington, myself and Gilbert Parkinson, in that order set off with a flourish. It was not long before I, with my very powerful OEC, overtook Henry Sutton and Fred Remington and I was continuing at high speed through Grayrigg, where I came across a corner liberally covered with wet leaves. These can be disastrous to a single track vehicle at high speed, so I set my wheels right against the bottom of the grassy bank to prevent side slip, this was successful in keeping me in control but my cap had blown off, so I went back to retrieve it. By this time some of the others should have caught me up but they didn't, so I returned to Grayrigg just in time to see Dicky Chaplow going into the Post Office. I said, "What's to do, Dicky? He replied, "Jack Robinson has had a bad accident, hit a double telephone pole and is badly injured, I am going to telephone for an ambulance."

He was in hospital for many months and eventually left hospital minus an arm and a leg. He had previously been a promising motor mechanic with Craghill & Co Ltd but there was no prospect of his ever resuming that kind of employment, so he was set up in a shop across the road from Craghills Garage selling sweets, tobacco, magazines and newspapers. He had a car adapted for him, he married and had two sons.

The Blackburne unfortunately proved to be unsuitable for the purpose for which I had bought it. On the road it was as near perfection as one can get for the purpose for which it was presumably designed; but it proved to be virtually unsteerable on steep 'rough stuff'. Under these conditions it was so very light on the steering, strangely enough this did not apply when descending the same rough stuff.

I remember in the 1928 Alan Trophy Trial when descending the east side of Wrynose (as it was in 1928), Faye Taylor the official Rudge Trials Rider, passed me at such a speed that I had previously considered to be impracticable. I immediately decided that if Faye Taylor could hang on to her Rudge Ulster model at that speed down here, so could I and I went after her. She gave me a riding lesson that I never forgot, so fast in fact that in the 1930 Sporty Boys Trial, I went from the bottom gate on the west side of Walna Scar to Coniston Station railway bridge on the GTP, 250cc, Velocette, in fifteen minutes and sixteen seconds. The descent of the Coniston side was pretty dreadful in 1930, at every previous check Len Ellwood on his works prepared 350cc, ohv, New Imperial, had arrived before I had left but on this occasion he had not. I was told by Louis Handley, who was in charge of the Coniston check that Len remarked, "I don't know where Bernard has got to?" He was amazed when Louis told him I had gone through, 'more than five minutes ago!' Len never rode in another trial to my knowledge. He had previously ridden that bike in the International Six Days' Trial for New Imperial, when it was run chiefly in Wales.

The following year 1931, I decided, with the help of my brother Malcolm, to build myself a new bike and, after the usual thought and paperwork stages, drawings etc, decided that I could build a machine with two 172cc Villiers Super Sports engines complete with magnetos and carburettors and coupled to a Moss four-speed gearbox, to which I fitted a Velocette foot change, with the mechanism suitably modified to work with a four-speed gearbox. The entire engine and gearbox unit was mounted in a steel subframe cut out of $\frac{3}{16}$ inch steel plate and the whole outfit, to work out with an overall length, the same as a GTP Velocette, which I had found to be easy to handle.

Having decided upon all aspects of requirements, I set to work by first ordering the parts I would require. I was twenty years of age and Malcolm was fifteen, so obviously I was responsible. He had been a good help to me in 1930 when I was moderately successful with the GTP Velocette. I appreciated the fact that whenever I returned from a trial, grass-track or scramble, he would take the bike from me as soon as I got back and hose it down. After I came back from the Baker Scramble, held on a new course at the back of Whinfell, he came to me and said, "Did you know your frame is broken?" To which I said, "No!" I immediately went to look at it, sure enough the nearside fork was broken off where it joined the fitting into which it was brazed and which supported the gearbox. I said to Malcolm, "No wonder my back chain kept coming off!" That was why I had to retire. I had been leading the field until it came off the first time but I refitted the chain and was still in front when off it came again. I retired, in the belief that the chain was twisted and I rode the bike back to Kendal very gingerly, in case it decided to come off again - it did not! I stripped the bike right down to the frame and cleaned it. I went down to Kit Parker's with it first thing Monday morning, I showed it to Kit who was surprised and he sent it back to Velocette that day. The bike was still in its six months guarantee period it was replaced without question of course, scrambling was not mentioned!

Now on a different tack! The next outing was something of a disaster. I was competing in a grass-track event put on by the Whitehaven Club - proceeds in aid of the local hospital and we were all invited to make this a good money raiser for the hospital. I can't remember who was there beyond Frank Allison from Brough, he was riding a 500cc, ohv, AJS. I won my heat, as did Frank, who also won his final. When I was turning out for the 350cc final, Frank said, "Where's your hat Bernard?" To which I replied, "I haven't one!" He then said, "Here, take mine!" That proved to be a life saver for me. The heats had been five laps and the finals were ten laps. I passed all the entries but one rider on a 350cc, ohv, Cotton, which I caught but could not pass because whenever he heard me coming up behind, he balked me over and over again by swinging to the same side, thus cutting me off. I kept trying but on the final lap I decided to try another way by coming up on his right and as soon as he began to swerve to cut me off, I was ready and prepared to change to the inside and was actually alongside, when his rear chain came off, his wheel locked and he was thrown over the handlebars right in front of me, I ran over him and landed on my head. Frank's crash hat was flattened. We both ended up in the hospital for which we were trying to raise funds! Neither of us regained consciousness until the following morning.

A Mr Kessel, who worked for a leading oil company and lived in

Whitehaven, looked after my interests and took me back to Kendal in his car on my release from hospital. I had not a particle of skin on the left side of my face, from my high cheekbone to my chin. I could not understand this, so I asked Mr Kessel how that had happened and he told me that they had put a lot of sand on the track to improve the grip, it did not improve my face! There was a mark on my face for many years but it disappeared over time. My Velocette was taken back to Ambleside on Harry Skirrow's trailer after the event and I collected it from there some days later in a van. I would not have been able to write this chapter of events, had they not been faithfully related to me later by Mr Kessel, who described what had happened in detail.

Returning to the bike my brother Malcolm and I were building, I placed orders for the steering head, taper roller bearings and the headstock spindle, plus the rear fork ends I would require for the proposed new bike from OEC. From Webb I ordered suitable forks for the nineteen inch diameter front wheel and the largest brakes they were making at that time for front and rear wheels. I ordered wheel rims from Dunlop for the 3.25 front tyre and the 3.50 rear tyre; spokes (blank) from R Cadisch & Sons, together with clean pattern handlebars from Sackville Ltd and tyres from our own stock. The petrol and oil tank was made to my design in Coventry, by the BBF Company. I had seen their name on a cinema screen when I was taking a course at the Armstrong Siddeley factory. The frame tubing was Reynolds top quality and all the other work was carried out in our own well-equipped workshops.

Originally there were two chains running in the oil bath chain case - one between the two engines and the other from the front engine to the gearbox - the former having a Weller type chain tensioner below the lower run of the chain. As most people know, two-stroke engines are not noted for their smooth tick-over and it was this 'flutter' that I was trying to prevent by the use of a tensioner; unfortunately, in the long run, it proved to be not very satisfactory.

I had done a few hundred miles on the new bike when along came the old type 'Sporty Boys Trial' including all the old terrors like Walna Scar. Three intrepid motorcyclists turned up for the 1pm start. It was midsummer and a pouring wet day - one of the worst. We three, myself, Foster Williamson and John Bower turned up at the start at the bottom of Kent Street, where we found Dicky Chaplow sheltering under the wall of Gilbert Parkinson's motorcycle shop, like a drowned rat and a face as long as a fiddle. He said, "I don't know what we are going to do, only you three turned up and the start is in five minutes. All the observers are out, over the far side of Walna Scar!" We three looked at each other and we all chimed in, "We will go round the whole course, starting in the mud at Whinfell and tell them all the trial is off!"

We did just that and mighty pleased they were to be relieved of their task. Our bikes were Sunbeam, Ariel and BAC respectively. We all got up as far as the upper gate on the west side of Walna where I went on a bit and, looking round, saw that I was not being followed, so I went back down as far as the gate and found John Bower pushing Foster Williamson up the steep grass slope and when he got to the top of that steep rise he waved his hand and kept going. Then John had a go and he could get no further than Foster had done, so I gave him a hand and he got to the top of the very steep bit and was coming back to give me a push but I was already on my way, which I put down to the very even torque of the twin two-engine stroke, which I had throttled right down to literally a tick-over and, at that very low speed, I had sufficient traction to climb the steep bank. We went round all the course including the forest sections and all were relieved at our appearance. Naturally we, in spite of our up to the minute all-weather gear, discovered that five hours in that deluge found its weak spots. In spite of all that we enjoyed the trip immensely, Laura ran me a hot bath as soon as she saw me, after which I was on top of the world.

A few weeks later I wanted to go to Craghills for some spare parts, I got the bike out, turned the petrol on, set the control and gave it one of my lunging kicks. It fired immediately on the front cylinder and stopped dead, I put the bike back on its stand and went in a car. It wasn't until the evening that I had a chance to have a look at it. I took the front cylinder off and everything seemed alright there, so then I took the rear one off, what a mess - the connecting rod was bent and a piece broken off the piston skirt. I decided immediately what I was going to do, take the intermediate primary chain off and ride it down to Villiers at Wolverhampton and let them sort it out. The cause of the problem was due to the fact that these two engines were fitted with the Villiers pressure lubrication system which, it transpires, was creating problems for them to the extent that they abandoned the whole system and went back to petroil lubrication. In actual fact this is how it worked; pressure was taken from the crankcases to the oil supply tanks, where pressure built up in the tanks, which in turn pushes oil down an adjustable sight feed to the front of the crankcase where, in order to stop the oil flowing when the engine stops, the pressure built up in the tanks was released through a microscopic hole drilled in the side of the individual sight feeds. In this case the oil sight feed to the rear cylinder was blocked. Villiers treated me very well - they were very taken up with the design and even said,

Bernard - Walna Scar 1930 on 250cc Velocette.

Bernard - bottom of Stoney Lane on 250cc Velocette 'Sporty Boys' 1930

"We could do with a few more like you, who would put two engines in every machine!"

Their next engine, the popular 197cc, was lubricated by the petroil system 16:1. They fitted a new crankshaft assembly and piston in the rear engine and a new piston in the front engine - it had partly seized on the way to Wolverhampton - all dealt with free of charge. I was happy and so were they. I later used the machine extensively but it was not very fast and it would have been pushed to reach sixty. It would however climb the steepest of hills, possibly due to the help of the Moss four-speed gear.

As I explained earlier, the machine with two 172cc Villiers engines had a Weller type chain tensioner beneath the lower run of the chain linking the two engines, which wore out (far too early in my opinion) and consequently left a lot of chain 'flutter'. I studied this carefully and had not come up with a solution, until it came to me in the middle of the night when I awoke and acted upon it immediately. I took out the rear engine, thank goodness all the holes were symmetrical, so that even when it was turned 'back to front' the cylinder was still vertical, as can be seen on photographs I have of the original design. I used only one carburettor on a chrome plated manifold, linking the two inlet ports but this obviously was no longer possible. So I got the other carburettor (which came with the engine) and fitted it to the rear engine, then made new exhaust pipes for the back to front engine with the engine now fitted in reverse, the magneto would not produce a spark. After spending a lot of time puzzling over this problem, I finally found that by moving the magneto into a new position in relation to the contact breaker cam it worked. I now had the drive problem which I had already solved in my mind right from beginning the change round. I discarded the chain linking the two engines and the weller chain tensioner and ran a new chain from the top of the gearbox sprocket, over the sprocket on the crankshaft of the front engine then under the sprocket and over the sprocket on the rear engine, thence under the clutch sprocket and joining with the chain at the point I began - the top of the clutch sprocket. It was a total success and ran without trouble and smoothly for thousands of miles. The chain was easily but rarely needed to be repositioned by sliding the four stud base mounted gearbox back slightly, then readjusting the final drive chain slightly. Actually, it was a very nice machine to ride - very smooth and easy to handle, although its top speed was only about 60mph. It climbed hills easily and, unless one was climbing Walna, first gear was seldom used.

As I have already said, Kit Parker was a particularly good friend and one day, when I called on him on the two-engined bike, he showed great interest in it and asked me how it performed. I told him what I have already said here and he asked, "Why didn't I consider the fitting of a twin-cylinder Scott engine?" I had never even thought of this and in any case the power take off of the Scotts I had been acquainted with was between the two cylinders and therefore unsuitable for using in conjunction with the gearboxes that were available to me on the market. He informed me that they had made a few twins of novel design with four bearing crankshafts (500 & 650cc), he then suggested that I should go over to Saltaire and see what they could offer. I did just that and came back with a 650cc engine complete. This of course set me thinking so I sold the 344cc twin-engined model and drew up plans for a suitable frame for the 650cc unit.

I designed a new frame and, having regard to the successful frame already made, I designed it on similar lines and again used the same kind of frame fittings with just a little longer wheelbase and this was in 1932. I again used a similar method of constructing the engine/gearbox/magneto unit - in fact when the sub-frame was fully assembled it was possible to start the engine and run it for a very short period (it was water-cooled, so could not run for more than a very short time without water).

Kit Parker had set my mind on further machine building, so I set about it in much the same manner I had done before, obtaining parts from the same manufacturers/suppliers I had used previously. The principal differences were that I used heavier gauge tubing for the frame, having regard to the much more powerful 650cc engine and the rather longer frame. A similar design of frame was used and a similar method of accommodating the engine and gearbox in a subframe made (cut out of) $\frac{3}{16}$" thick steel plate, with a duplicate (twin-tube) seat pillar. In this case, there was no flywheel magneto involved or carburettor supplied. I ordered a BTH magdynamo only because this was not as tall as the Lucas alternative and fitted with ample clearance under the offside frame tube. The carburettor I ordered was from Amal (I was surprised to receive this item by return of post). Amal must have put a number of these carburettors into production - anticipating more orders to follow - which unfortunately did not materialise as production of that engine was not proceeded with. On both machines, I found the building of the wheels to be the most tiresome, not even knowing what length to cut the spokes, it was a question of cutting them on the long side and then recutting until the correct length was established. This machine was also fitted with an oil bath primary chaincase, no fancy tensioners, simply moving the Moss gearbox as required for correct chain tension. No particular problems were encountered, although I took the machine over to Saltaire to show to Scott's. I had a cousin, Miss Ethel Ashworth, who came to Kendal from Hebden Bridge and worked in our office for a good many years. She had recently bought a new 150cc Sheffield Dunelt Villiers and when she knew I was riding to Saltaire, she asked if she could accompany me, and naturally I agreed. I accompanied her all the way and then made my way back to Saltaire. I had already noticed that there was vibration beginning to occur in the engine, which was much more noticeable when I was crawling alongside Ethel and, on the return journey, again with Ethel, it continued to worsen. I could not at the time imagine the cause, so when I got back, I took out the engine and dismantled it fully. I found the cause, the result of 'crawling' in too high a gear - the flywheel was riveted to a central flange on the crankshaft and the rivets had come loose. I fitted a new set of rivets and made certain they were well riveted - never any further trouble! I forgot to mention that I made the all-steel fully welded petrol and oil tank. The duplex Pilgrim oil pump was attached to the outer cover of the oil bath chaincase. The footrests I used for this machine were Velocette. (This is the motorcycle on which Malcolm was tragically killed). After I sold it, as I said earlier, I continued to know it quite intimately for the next two owners. After that I lost track of it and in fact have never heard of it since. Being a Scott engine it was water-cooled and I made a wooden mock-up of the radiator I would require and a honeycomb radiator was made exactly to these dimensions by Serck Radiators, Carlisle branch. They repaired many radiators for us in our line of business and fitted new tube blocks etc. The bike was certainly never returned to us for any repair or maintenance work, even though the name of our firm as manufacturers was painted on the horizontal surface of the rear number plate.

I later bought a 250cc Dot Scrambler and converted it for road use. When we went to live in Malta, I sent this forward by sea. I didn't use it very much on the Island, Laura - who had been an enthusiastic motorcyclist (pillion) only went on it the once in Malta and although I did use it a bit, it was not much fun by myself, so I sold it. Next time we came to England I saw a Greeves Scottish advertised, it was just up the road and I bought it for about £50. Having put it into usable condition I sold it to a mechanic at Victrix Motor Works in Kendal. My motorcycling days were finished, I thought!

I have omitted one interlude in 1950. I bought a 197cc Villers-engined OEC and used it a bit in trials. My friend Percy Harris offered to prepare it for scrambles and I provided the bike, fuel and oil. Any prizes

1932 BAC 650cc water cooled engine. Shows gearbox platform, Moss 4-speed gear, crankcase 'split' exposing crankshaft and flyweel - also sub-frame which requires only four ⅜" diameter through bolts to instal the complete unit.

Close-up of engine.

Percy won he kept, he had the fun riding it - I was past scrambling. We had fun, we used to take the bike all over in our Morris 'S' type van and it - the van - was never any trouble, its side-valve engine used to scream with joy when we really got going. How Percy managed to see to ride the bike with his eyes bunged up with mud - I shall never know! After removing the cylinder alloy head, I welded up the inside head area, made a jig to which I could fit it for matching of the combustion space and fitted a large Amal carburetter prepared for methanol. The carb was mounted direct on to the inlet port, I cleaned up all the ports and shortened the piston slightly, using methanol for fuel, (using methanol demands vegetable oil) - so Castrol R it had to be, we were very successful semi-locally and now wish we had been more ambitious and gone further afield. Being in the motor trade took me into the Midlands from time to time, and on one of these trips I made it my business to call on Villiers and have a chat with their competitions' manager as I wanted to know how I could get even more power out of it. He asked me what I had done already and when I told him we were running with 13:1 compression ratio on methanol fuel and Castrol R and that I was riding the same machine with a standard cylinder head and 16:1 Castrol XL! in petrol, he was horrified! He simply could not believe it. How did we make the change from methanol/Castrol R: to Petrol Castrol XL: I told him no problem. We just drained the tank changed the cylinder head and carburettor, then put the petrol/mineral oil in the tank and started the engine on a fast tickover and vice-versa, when we were changing to methanol/Castrol R, we never experienced any lubrication problems and did it go?!

I later decided to go further and again welded the combustion space and machined out to a compression ratio of 15:1. As this did not improve the performance further, I again removed the head and put it back to 13:1. I did not mention that I milled a space 1" wide across the fins (transversely) into which space I let in, 1" x ¼" steel plate through which the cylinder head bolts passed. We never experienced any leakage from the head joint.

Eventually, during a scramble which Percy was leading by a very considerable margin, when coming down the long straight on the easiest and fastest part of the course, it suddenly developed a most alarming misfire. He had to retire as it could not climb the next hill. A pity as up to that point it had been leading the way. Percy is a first class mechanic in his own right and (so am I for that matter) unfortunately it occurred during the busiest part of the year for us (and for Percy). However, I devoted as much time to it as I could spare, even tried another flywheel

Percy Harris on a Matchless Scrambler on Lindeth - 1950s.

Percy Harris

John and Michael Airey on Parade on Mayor's Sunday, Kendal about 1956.
Car was made as a gimmick by a leading manufacturer and they borrowed the trade plates from the garage.

magneto - all without any noticeable result.

Percy came round at the end of the first week to see what results I had and I rather ashamedly admitted that I had not had any success. Percy then said do you mind if I take it to my garage and have a go at it - I said not at all and the best of luck. Towards the end of the week he brought it back and admitted that he had had no better results than I.

On the Saturday, Bob Mason, not a motor mechanic, but who knew his way around motorcycles, came in and asked if we had got it right? I said, "Unfortunately, no." He said, "Do you mind if I take it and have a go at it?" Literally I was quite fed up with it, being so busy in the garage with our regular work, I could not afford to spend any more time on it so I let Bob take it. He said he had an arrangement with a farmer to use some of his fields and he could test it under scramble conditions. He brought it back a few days later and said it was better. It was already entered for a scramble at Skipton, so we took it there in the van, and it seemed to go fairly well in the first heat but, come the final, it was back at its old tricks, so an appeal was put over the loud speaker to enquire if anyone with a 197 Villiers engined bike would lend his flywheel magneto. A young man came across to us with a 197 Ambassador and he offered to lend us his magneto if we would put it back again after the scramble, which we hastily agreed to do, and in fact we did. It was not the slightest bit better. Up to that point, I had been considering buying a new orthodox magneto, mounting it on a plate above the cylinder head and driving it with a chain from the opposite side of the machine. The end of the season was now upon us (almost) and we were still very busy, the bike was put to one side, and lo and behold a young man came in, gave it a short run up the road paid his money and took it away. We had lost our high compression cylinder head, large carburettor and special exhaust pipe. We simply gave over scrambling at that point. I still wonder and often think we ought to have had another go! We are all past it now! In 1950 we were paying less than £200 for a new 197cc Villiers, what price today - if one could be bought?

Now to my motoring days in the club. I earned something of a reputation as a trials driver with MG cars, the then president of the Westmorland Motor Club once told me that he considered me to be the best trials driver in the north of England! I think Bill Pearce, the Rootes Representative who used to call on us, must have heard of this because once in the course of conversation he asked me if I had ever thought of writing to Norman Garrard the manager of the Sunbeam Talbot Alpine Team. I never did, we were far too busy at that time.

When Laura and I were married in 1934, my car at that time was an

'M' type MG. We went in a few car trials and were moderately success-ful against newer cars. Our next car was a 'PA' type MG, after that we had a 'TA' type and we had three of these in succeeding years. Each car had done around 10,000 miles and we became the most prolific winners in the car section of the Westmorland Motor Club in 1936, 1937 and 1939. We did not compete in 1938, Laura was heavily pregnant with our daughter and we thought it best to abstain. You will understand why after reading the next section.

It is remarkable how things one has never thought possible occur! It would probably be in 1934 or early 1935 that Jim Lafone, accompanied by Dick Heaton from Prizet, came into the garage with a sorry tale to tell. Dick Heaton had taken Jim over Wrynose Pass in his 'PA' type MG and they were going down Wrynose bottom and were not very far from reaching the bridge over Cockley Beck, when Jim, as was his wont, was encouraging Dick to get a move on and he had a habit of repeating this. The net result was that after rounding a few bends the inevitable happened, one corner they approached was sharper than those already negotiated, with the inevitable result that they would 'run out of road', which is precisely what they did. The car shot off the road and landed some four yards away on the top of a rocky hillock. It was quite literally stuck there. I don't know how they got back, that was something I did not enquire about, the fact was they had come to me to retrieve the car. I took the breakdown vehicle and, with planks and the crane, I was able to get it off the rocky hillock and back on to the roadway and into our garage. The insurance assessor duly came to examine it and he asked for offers for the salvage. There was much damage underneath, especially to the chassis, as it was bent upwards in the middle. I put in an offer for the salvage on the firm's notepaper and wonder of wonders, it was accepted. I don't know what Dick Heaton did for a car after that, but here was a chance for me to update my transport at modest cost, as it was mainly lots of labour, rather than material that were required for restoration.

Laura took a keen interest in the restoration and came in the evenings to give me a hand. This car, when completely restored, took us over Summer Lodge Moor, Park Rash (Yorkshire Moors), and other places of motoring interest. I sold the car very well, which later helped me to buy a new 'T series' MG which of course I got at cost price and, when I sold that one after only a season's use, it was in better than new condition due to genuine improvements I had made and it didn't even have a scratch.

By this time we were having trials of a sterner nature which involved keeping time and observation, and crossing from the bottom of Dent

Austin 7 struggling up Summer Lodge Moor in Yorkshire and the crowds watching - 1940s

Bottom of Park Rash - Bernard, Laura and the Bower family

Station Hill right over the moor, through all the sheep pens to Garsdale Station, opening and closing all the gates on the way. This included Laura being ready to jump out at every gate, letting me through with the car, and closing the gate after me. With the sheep pens, this involved Laura in jumping out to open each gate, dashing through and closing the gate, then sitting on the outside of the door edge, with feet on the running board (an extension of the front wing), she hung on to the windscreen frame, jumping off and opening the next gate, allowing me to pass through with the car and closing the gate again afterwards. I think there were three or possibly four of such sheep pens. All this was done at an average speed of 24mph. No other competitor in the three years referred to, achieved this without losing penalty points on time. It was not an observed section but it was timed for the whole length! Laura was marvellous in this manoeuvre and I believe unsurpassed certainly by any of the other competitors.

On another 'earlier occasion' I was driving a 'PB' Midget (taken in from Dr Rothwell) against a new, 2 litre MG saloon. The 'PB' had just had four new 4.00 x 19 Dunlop Fort tyres fitted (a bonus). The start of the Trial was from the hotel at the head of the Little Langdale valley. As I was and am still a teetotaller, I seldom frequented pub bars but I went into the bar before starting time and one of the organisers and a number of competitors were standing there with their drinks and it seems they had been asking what the course was like. The response was, well you know what the Tilberthwaite Quarry sections are like, no-one will finish without loss of marks on time - I walked on. I was the only competitor not to lose marks on time. The penalty for this was the visible amount of tread pattern removed from the tyres - fronts particularly! Ron Booth was the man talking in the bar, I happened to be passing when he was 'holding forth.'

Similarly, on another occasion, Tommy Turner had marked out the course. I overheard him telling two competitors that no-one would complete the course without losing marks on time - I kept on walking. I didn't say a word but made a mental note. I warmed my engine up again prior to being called to start, my car had an additional expansion chamber which I had made and it was fitted before with the standard Burgess Silencer and it had the effect of reducing the exhaust noise in some measure. The start was at one minute intervals and when I was given the signal to start, I began at a very modest pace and fairly silently but immediately over Miller Bridge, I gave it the gun and actually got up to 70mph on an almost deserted Aynam Road at 1pm. I got down to the first observed section at Mabbin Hall, south of Levens Bridge - narrow, stoney and overgrown hedges at both sides, thence forward I made haste everywhere, using my powerful vacuum horn frequently on the twisted and unfamiliar road. The net result was I was the only car not to lose a single mark thoughout the trial on time.

At the committee meeting the next Monday evening, Tom Turner openly accused me of cutting sections out of the course. Without knowing the course this would have been impossible, the course only having been marked with red dye just before the start. In the meeting, I punctured his outburst by saying I would take him round the course and offered to bet him £10 that I could do it again - he didn't take me on. This was the second time I had been challenged thus but in neither case would they take me on.

On another occasion various clubs in the northern centre had a 'do' at a pub at Troutbeck in Cumberland. It was beginning to get a bit out of hand, so some of us decided to leave. Hubert Trickett and his lady friend left about ten minutes before my wife and I. When we regained the main road on the west bank of Ullswater and were approaching the county boundary when, upon descending a hill with a right hand bend, we saw a car in the Lake. It was Hubert Trickett's and fortunately, although the car had jumped several yards over the Lake, it was not in deep water. It was late at night and the passengers were safe; so we went out with the breakdown vehicle first thing the following morning, Sunday, taking with us chain blocks, chains and ropes. I had already taken stock of the situation late the previous night. We had also taken a ladder, and a sling chain and hung it round a large branch jutting over the Lake, upon which the chain blocks were hung. Ropes were then put round the car and it was lifted bodily out of the water and dragged on to the road, which was a good three feet higher than the water level. We got it back to Kendal and, after changing all the oils and the acid in the batteries and a thorough lubrication job, it was not much the worse. That model MG ('PA' type) did not have hydraulic brakes. The towing to Kendal was by tow bar (not rope) as we had to cross Kirkstone Pass and it was considered not to be safe to use a rope on that occasion, although I don't think towing by means of a rope was illegal at that time (1936).

In a 1937 Car Trial, Laura and I had made good time and the skies looked as if they could open at any minute. We pulled off the road on the left side to put up the hood on our 'TA' type MG. Whilst we were doing this the club president, J H Lafone, pulled in just in front of us. He didn't think it was going to rain but I replied that we were ahead of time and did not want to take any chances in the car. With Mr Lafone were Bill Montgomery and Roger Moser. Jim said, "We are a bit pushed

Cat Hole Inn, Keld, where WMC conducted trials and used to halt for teas with home cured ham - pre-second world war.
Left to right: Laura, Cecil O'Loughlin, L K Brownson (stripes), two not known, Guy Bower, Ron Booth, J H Bower, F Brennand and R D Humber.

Cars parked outside the Inn.

for time (he was an earlier number) so we will press on." His car, I should mention, was a 'VA' series MG, open four-seater tourer. About halfway down the western side of Wrynose the heavens opened and, under instruction by Jim, they tried to erect the four-seater hood, without the preliminary of stopping the car, the result was that the forward pace of the car, plus the wind almost had Bill and Roger right out of the car. The hood went up vertically. We were still behind and saw all this but they had not had enough yet, so they made another attempt with the same result. The car was then stopped because they could not by this time erect the hood or even put it away - the wind, rain and motion saw to that, we were later informed. They were very late and very wet at the next check.

Now in another similar case; this was a Chain Gang Frazer Nash owned by Jack Hutton and his wife. (Chain Gang - was the nickname given - separate chain for each gear engaged by the dog clutch). This time was on another car trial, us in our 'TA' type MG and Jack and Noreen in their Chain Gang Frazer Nash. This trial took us from Whinlatter Pass and down the western side of Honister Pass. When we caught up with Jack and Noreen, they were making good progress, as indeed we had due to the narrowness of the track and, in the interests of safety, we quite simply had to stay behind. We hadn't been behind them very long when the wind got hold of the hood material on Jack's car and ripped it off right across the top of the windscreen, it went vertically into the air, where it remained flapping horribly.

After the second world war the club got going again. My father had died and thus couldn't hold the fort for me whilst we were competing so we had to call it a day. Laura had undoubtedly been responsible for our earlier success, she was a marvellous passenger and completely unflappable.

As a result of the accident that happened to Mr Hutchinson, when he was trapped against the garage wall as a result of the self-changing gearbox fitted in his car when he forgot to leave his car in neutral, before starting it with a starting handle. As a member of the committee of the club, I tried to get cars with fluid flywheels and automatic clutches banned from competing in the annual flexibility trial, the club used to organise on the 'Greyhound', a steep hill leaving Kendal on the Sedbergh Road. This trial consisted of a measured distance to be travelled, firstly in the longest time possible, and then to make the fastest time possible over the next section of the same length. An observer was carried in the cars to ensure that no driver touched his clutch pedal and motorcyclists were checked by observers, who covered the distance of the 'slow section'. The person with the greatest time difference being adjudged the winner. My motion was defeated, so I entered an Armstrong Siddeley 17, with Newton clutch and won the car event. Shortly after that, the Police banned the club from carrying out this test on the public road.

I cannot remember the names of all the regular competitors or their cars - but here are a few:- J H Bower - Singer 9; J Bewsher - Morgan J Z 1100cc, ohv, JAP; B Crabtree - MG 'TA'; K Blenkharn - Morris 8; B Holmes - MG 'VA'; J Ewart MG S2; H Ewart - Riley Imp; E Kerr - Alvis 1250cc; J H Lafore - MG 'VA'; G Grisedale - Morris 8; J Sancto - Citroen Super Modern 12; C O'Loughlin - BSA Scout; W Smith - Jaguar 2½ litre; T Turner - MG 'J2'; G Parkinson - Sunbeam Talbot; H Trickett - MG 'PA'; Geoff Lafone - Ford V8, G W Dodds - Singer 9; J Thompson - Austin A70 and R Riley - Riley 12.

Here is a list of some of the places we used for trials: Sadghyll, Garburn, Blea Tarn, Wrynose, Hardknott, Whinlatter, Honister and Rake Howe; the road from Matterdale over the top, through the ford into St Johns-in-the-Vale; Kirkstone Pass from Ambleside and from Patterdale; Gatesgarth from Long Sleddale to Haweswater; Park Rash, Summer Lodge and Tan Hill, in Yorkshire.

I had three 'TA' type MG cars in succeeding years, all were sold with just less than 10,000 miles on the clock and after about 8-10 months use for each of the cars. I later had an MGA to which I fitted a factory-prepared high compression cylinder head and aluminium rocker cover, it also had SU carburettors tuned for use with a mixture of alcohol, benzole and petrol, in the mixture 80-10-10. I entered the annual Barbon Open Hill Climb but only made a mediocre showing, although my young brother, Bryan, with the Marshall blown MG 'TB' which, unlike my MGA, he had prepared himself did better. It was a bit like riding on a shovel but my word it could go. He won the event in two successive years.

One week I took delivery of a new MG on the Wednesday and we went on an all-night trial to Scarborough. Driving a new car in a trial was not too bad for a new car, driven carefully, but when we reached Scarborough they (the WMC), decided to run an impromptu sand race at Saltburn (where the sands are frequently used for this purpose). One of the Committee had taken timing apparatus, a member of our staff, a salesman, had asked permission to use a second hand MG Magnette for the trial. We agreed and when the sand race was proposed he asked permission to use the car in the sand race. I gave him permission and I then went to the party organising the race and asked permission for me to use the same car in the race, pointing out that it was our car and that as my car was only delivered to me new on Wednesday, I had no wish to do it harm by racing it so soon in its life. Permission was granted in the circumstances. I went last after all the others had had their runs, guess what, I made fastest time of the day, our salesman was second fastest. He came to me afterwards and asked how I had made the car go faster than he had been able to - I simply said, "A more experienced driver!"

After helping Mr D H Delamont, the RAC competitions' manager, to organise a course in our area he mentioned the fact of me applying to be an RAC Scrutineer and it would save the Westmorland Motor Club money. I did just that and was appointed and duly served the WMC as scrutineer at no cost for many years. During those years, I also officiated as scrutineer at various events in North Wales, Liverpool, Blackpool, Morecambe, Harewood, Carlisle, Kirkbride, Ouston, Penrith, Leighton Hall and Barbon - many at annual events.

Alan Spencer or Dick Mashiter assisted in the more recent years when the number of competitors was reaching saturation level. Generally we had no trouble and those who objected to our ruling generally complied with our instructions when they saw that we were inflexible. We had a very cordial relationship with competitors who came to the events year after year. I thoroughly enjoyed it over the twelve years I officiated.

Our late president of the WMC once said to me, "I think you must be one of the best drivers in the north of England." I must admit I had some success and thoroughly enjoyed every minute of those years.

Bernard as Chairman of the WMC presenting a trophy to Leslie Picthall at the Annual Dinner at the Low Wood Hotel in late 1940/50s

Bernard on the Bultaco 250cc on Hardnott, aged 62 years - before hats were compulsory.

Retirement and the end of Crabtree's

Peter, my son, had come home after serving his apprenticeship and spent a year in the family business. In 1967-68 Victrix Garage came on the market again when Billy Dickinson retired. We decided to buy the garage as it was too near us for active competition. The garage was auctioned and was bought equally between myself, my brother Bryan, Percy Harris and my son, Peter. Eventually Peter became the sole owner.

Unfortunately things did not work out and Peter came out of the garage. He later set up another business dealing in petrol pumps and is doing well. He has a daughter and two sons and I am now a great grandfather.

Meanwhile things were not going completely smoothly with us in the garage business. Laura took a down turn in health and collapsed in April 1969. Under doctor's orders we decided to seek a warmer climate and, after much thought, we bought a flat in Malta. In December 1973 I retired and we went to live out there permanently. We kept our house on at Moorfields and returned to England when it was too warm in Malta. We enjoyed seventeen happy years there together.

The garage was left solely in my brother Bryan's hands, though I did keep my fifty per cent share in it for about eight years. Things gradually went downhill caused by a number of reasons and the business folded and Crabtree's was no more.

We eventually returned to England from Malta on our doctor's advice, in December 1989. Laura lived five years after we came back to Kendal - not to Moorfields because of the steps but we took a ground floor flat at 16 Websters Yard, in the middle of Kendal. Laura was taken to hospital on 1st January 1995 and sadly died there on 15th February of that year. We had been married sixty years and I miss her greatly.

My daughter lives at Moorfields now with my granddaughter Gillian. I myself am now a resident at Summerhill in Kendal and in my nineties. I am not as active and sadly had to give up driving a number of years ago.

I hope you enjoy reading about my life, filled with motor cycles, cars and engines and have learned a little about these early pioneering years in our old grey town!

Bernard with Martin Proctor and the Hillman car that Martin still proudly owns and displays at vintage car shows, winning many prizes, Summerhill, Kendal on 15th August 2000

Christine Moore (Bernard's daughter)

HILLMAN, HUMBER
SUNBEAM-TALBOT
& M.G. CARS
MORRIS COMMERCIAL VEHICLES
D.M.W. AND O.E.C.
LIGHTWEIGHT MOTOR CYCLES

Z. Crabtree & Co
LIMITED

TELEPHONE
KENDAL 190
TELEGRAMS
CRABTREES KENDAL

MOTOR AGENTS AND ENGINEERS

OLDHAM BATTERY SERVICE STATION

KIRKLAND

KENDAL

M.Proctor, Esq.,
Railway Terrace,
Lowgill. Westmorland.

20th. July,1960.

1960.

July 20			£	s.	d.
	To	Hillman de Luxe Saloon complete to manufacturers specification and warranty, finished Regency Beige/Caramel and fitted with centre floor type gear shift. Including purchase tax.......	778	17	6
	"	Delivery charges ex works.	8	10	-
	"	Bluemels lightweight aluminium number plates.	2	10	-
	"	Overiders- front and rear.	4	10	-
	"	Leopard Kumficar Loose Covers fitted.	17	10	-
	"	Pye Em TCR 2000 Touch Button radio, complete with installation kit and fully retractable 4 pull aerial and including fitting charge.	32	19	-
	"	Undersealing car throughout.	10	10	-
	"	Heater with blower, complete installation.	20	10	-
	"	Making special brackets to support owners Lucas large size twin lamp set, fitting lamps and wiring up. Making special brackets for reverse lamp, fitting lamp and wiring up. Fitting wheel trims, oil gauge kit, ammeter etc.	4	5	-
	"	Reverse Lamp Switch.		9	-
	"	11 yds. Wiring cable.		8	9
	"	Licence.	6	11	3
	"	Wheel trims.	5	-	-
	"	Oil gauge.	2	15	-
	"	Ammeter.		15	6
			£ 896	1	-

B1069192 HSO.

14630

KIRKLAND GARAGE.
KENDAL.

........................19 £ s. d.

CASH

Received with thanks from CHEQUE

....

....

Per Z. CRABTREE & Co. Ltd.

....

Bill for Hillman car purchased by Martin Proctor in 1960.

161

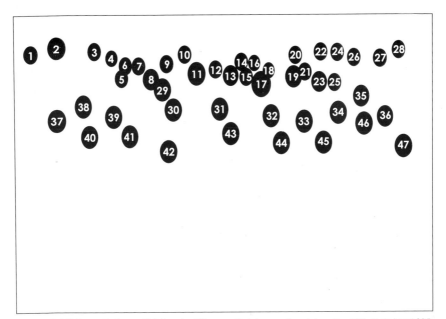

'Black Tie' Veteran Motorcyclists lunch at Heaves Hotel, near Kendal on the 19th October 1995 (Bernard's 87th birthday)

Black ties are worn three times a year to remember a motorcycling legend of the past and to celebrate his/her life and achievements.

Courtesy of the Westmorland Gazette

1. Miles Newton	17. Cyril Scott	32. Eva Humble
2. Robin Clinch	18. Phil Bowker	33. Ella McCrone
3. Harry Holme	19. Alan Johnson	34. Kath Scaife
4. Frank Scaife	20. Dick Haugh	35. Don Butterworth
5. Angus Tyson	21. Roger Mallinson	36. Ronnie Riley
6. Jack Wilson	22. Ron Pears	37. Alan Smith
7. Billy Wilson	23. Alan Todd	38. Ray Holme
8. Ken Marshall	24. Brian Elleray	39. Eleanor Watson
9. Percy Harris	25. Bob Humble	40. Dorothy Fisher
10. Brian Smith	26. Bill Bewley	41. Percy Duff
11. David Stewart	27. Arthur Fogg	42. Margaret Duff
12. Jack Philipson	28. John Tallontire	43. Bernard (the author)
13. Joan Butterworth	29. Alec Edmondson	44. Kath Pears
14. Hugh Clifford	30. Peter Hetherington	45. Sheila Smith
15.	31. Christine (Bernard's daughter)	46. Malcolm Tyson
16. Les Passell		47. Maurice Newsham